Duty and Sentiment

Eiji Yamamura

Duty and Sentiment

How Culture Shapes Thinking and Behavior in Japan and the West

 Springer

Eiji Yamamura
Department of Economics
Seinan Gakuin University
Fukuoka, Japan

ISBN 978-981-16-9766-1   ISBN 978-981-16-9767-8 (eBook)
https://doi.org/10.1007/978-981-16-9767-8

Translation from the Japanese language edition: 義理と人情の経済学 by Eiji Yamamura, © 東洋経済新報社 2020. Published by 東洋経済新報社. All Rights Reserved.
© The Editor(s) (if applicable) and The Author(s), under exclusive license to Springer Nature Singapore Pte Ltd. 2022
This work is subject to copyright. All rights are solely and exclusively licensed by the Publisher, whether the whole or part of the material is concerned, specifically the rights of reprinting, reuse of illustrations, recitation, broadcasting, reproduction on microfilms or in any other physical way, and transmission or information storage and retrieval, electronic adaptation, computer software, or by similar or dissimilar methodology now known or hereafter developed.
The use of general descriptive names, registered names, trademarks, service marks, etc. in this publication does not imply, even in the absence of a specific statement, that such names are exempt from the relevant protective laws and regulations and therefore free for general use.
The publisher, the authors and the editors are safe to assume that the advice and information in this book are believed to be true and accurate at the date of publication. Neither the publisher nor the authors or the editors give a warranty, expressed or implied, with respect to the material contained herein or for any errors or omissions that may have been made. The publisher remains neutral with regard to jurisdictional claims in published maps and institutional affiliations.

'Madoi Bi' (A Day of Reflection) by Eiji Yamamura, (c) Eiji Yamamura

This Springer imprint is published by the registered company Springer Nature Singapore Pte Ltd.
The registered company address is: 152 Beach Road, #21-01/04 Gateway East, Singapore 189721, Singapore

Preface

How many of the readers remember Keizo Obuchi? He is a former prime minister of Japan, but I remember him more as a chief cabinet secretary who announced the regnal title of the new imperial era, "Heisei," holding up a frame bearing the title in calligraphy in a press conference. Years have gone by, and I am writing this in December 2018, the last year of the Heisei era.

Photo of Keizo Obuchi holding up a frame with the new imperial era, "Heisei". ©JIJI Press, Ltd.

Today, artificial intelligence is so advanced that it has surpassed human abilities. The world has evolved to the extent that someone like me, born in the 1960s, only knew it in science fiction. It is a world as surreal as the life in space we would watch in good old *Star Trek*. But now, it is progressively a matter of real life. For example, AI has beaten humans in abstract strategy board games, such as *shogi*, or Game of Generals, and "*go*." It makes me wonder whether this trend would eventually wipe out professional players in these games in the future. However, we do have professional chess players around despite that it has been more than twenty years since AI conquered a chess world champion. From another viewpoint, it is us humans, not the computer algorithm, who enjoy watching professional games of chess, *shogi*, *go*, etc. People do watch a board game match and enjoy something in it other than finding out who has won. Perhaps, this something is to do with living human beings in action. Humanity, in a broad sense of the word, is stimulating the demand for games between professional players. It is therefore not very far from the truth that, at the fundamental level, there lie human sentiments behind the ways in which society and economy function.

How about supply? Some predict that AI will take over half of the work carried out by humans today. However, what is essentially "artificial" cannot feel or understand emotions, and it is difficult for me to imagine that it will replace humans to do the jobs that require reading and responding to human emotions. There are cutting-edge projects to recreate emotions in AI. Some research attempts "to program AI to emulate human beings by giving it sophisticated emotive attributes, with a focus on facilitating the ability to communicate with real human beings."[1] Artificial intelligence needs humans to define a framework and feed a large volume of existing information for it to function, but the kind of "emotion" they try to make AI emulate is only an aggregate of human behaviors generated and generalized from the big data taken from the human world. However, we humans in real life draw on shared norms, cultural understanding, etc. without making conscious efforts, as human interaction requires responses that take into account the specific circumstances or contexts in which it occurs. Some time ago, an AI project became a center of attention in Japan. Named "Todai Robot Project," a group of researchers aimed to develop an AI robot that could pass an admission exam for Japan's most prestigious university, the University of Tokyo. According to the team leader Noriko Arai, however, the Todai Robot "will never be able to pass the exam"[2]. The reason for this conclusion is that the artificial intelligence lacks the ability to understand the context and read between the lines, and also a body of tacit knowledge with which we understand what is the norm. For AI to be able to function just like a living human being, it needs to learn about shared sense of the normal and culture through information, but such information would be enormously diverse and voluminous. Moreover, norms and cultures are time- and region-dependent, so there is not much advantage in gathering information globally via the Internet. In other words, there is a decisive insufficiency of the information that can be collected in a practical sense. The readers must not confuse the kind

---

[1] Kimura (2018: 97).

[2] Arai (2018).

of humanity I talk about simply with emotions. We shall define, for the sake of convenience, emotion to mean an intuitive mental response to a specific situation, event, etc. The sentimental humanity, which I occasionally refer to by the Japanese word "*ninjo*," is more like a mental disposition or a faculty of the human mind to feel emotions or determine enduring sentimental attitudes. Emotions are more or less universally observable in individuals, and the *ninjo* disposition is something that is fostered in people through their cultural and historical backgrounds. In the nature-culture dichotomy, emotions are like a biological attribute of the mind that all human beings are born with while the sentimental humanity is like a diverse, cultural attribute that is formed in relation to the environment of particular times and places.

This book is all about humanity that all humans with feelings are capable of having, and a sense of indebtedness combined with a self-imposed obligation for reciprocation, a sense to which the Japanese refer as "*giri*," which characterizes this book. It also features "sympathy" here and there as an important element, which is variable depending on geographical, temporal, and social conditions. It is important to know these aspects of humanity in the context of our everyday communication and, certainly, in economic activities. I have always been treating this as my research subject and conducting studies through various approaches, such as sports economics, economics of trust, education economics, and family economics. These studies are empirical, based on data collected from the real world, as opposed to laboratory-based studies, like ones in psychology. So, the intention behind this book is to present the knowledge gained from these studies to the general public.[3] A couple of examples will perhaps serve as good illustrations.

A chain noodle restaurant, Fujisoba, pays its employees more than their contributions to the company, and even part-timers are paid bonuses. The company's president was known to take out people who came for a job interview to buy them a meal. It may not make sense at all to spend money for someone who may or may not be working for the company in the future. It is a logical consequence that inflated non-essential cost will eventually bankrupt the company. However, Fujisoba is in fact doing rather well. This means that the apparent meaningless cost is in fact a meaningful investment—to "steal their hearts," so to speak. Employees are humans, not machines or robots. Job seekers are also individuals, only that they may not yet have made their minds up about this particular job opportunity. When a company treats them well, better than their expectations, they naturally feel that they owe a debt of gratitude to the company, which then translates into the sense of fealty and boosts their morale to work hard, to reciprocate the favor.

In the classic literature on Japanese culture and its behavioral principles *The Chrysanthemum and the Sword*, Ruth Benedict characterized Japan as being based on a "shame culture," in which people reacted to other people's opinions and disapproval of them, in contrast to the American "guilt culture," that operated on people's internalized absolute moral standards.[4] She refers to the notion of "*giri*" as a cultural

---

[3] For example, Levitt and Dubner (2006) and Gneezy and List (2014) are written in styles similar to the one adopted for this book.

[4] Benedict (1946).

pillar of the Japanese, juxtaposing it to the Ten Commandments: "The rules of giri are strictly rules of required repayment, they are not a set of moral rules of like the Ten Commandments" (Benedict 1946: Chap. 7). Has this cultural pattern that was explained in this 1946 literature survived all these years? I refer to a Harvard economist, Judd Cramer. This American economist is known in Japan not by his work, but by the action he chose to take. In 2019, an article about him was circulated on the Internet, that he was trying to locate a Japanese man who had helped him about 14 years before. His story begins from a trip to Japan to visit his Japanese friend from high school. When he reached the northern city of Sendai, a major earthquake hit the region, and he was stranded at a railway station. Being a foreign budget traveler, barely in his high teens and not speaking a word of Japanese, he was completely at loss, not knowing even how to find a bed for the night. Then, the young Cramer was rescued by "a station worker in his thirties or so, with only one arm" from Sendai Station. He took the American to a nearby hostel and paid the bill for him. The next day, this "one-armed" station worker saw Cramer's expired train ticket and issued a new ticket free of charge so that the poor traveler could be on his way home. This whole event left a profoundly deep impression in Cramer and changed the course of his life. He learned the Japanese language and culture, hoping one day to see the "one-armed station worker" and thank him "in the Japanese way." In 2019, Cramer came back to Japan in search of this man, but he could not find him at Sendai Station. He continues his search, determined to tell him "Thank you" in person. Standard economics cannot explain the behavior of either the station worker who willingly bore some cost in order to help a stranger whom he would probably never meet again, or an economist who spends time and effort to find the station worker to say, "thank you," knowing that there will be no economic return in his doing so. I believe that Cramer learned what significance indebtedness had for the Japanese through his experience in, and learning about, Japan. His behavior is, it seems to me, an enactment of the self-imposed obligation to repay the debt of gratitude, or in other words, acting on the "*giri*" principle.

Taking the humanity aspect into account means considering economy with reference to contexts of specific times and places. For this reason, this book is arranged with a particular awareness of the temporal axis in the Japanese context, a textured continuum from the past to the future. At the time of writing this manuscript, we live in the era of Heisei, and by the time the book is published, it will be an era with a new title. Crossing this threshold may mean very little to non-Japanese people, but it will have at least some impact on the lives of those who live in the country. The change of the regnal title will incur economic cost to some extent, for example, in updating administrative forms and procedures. Standard economics holds that inefficient systems will be abandoned in favor of efficient systems through selection. Then, why on earth does Japan maintain the Japanese calendar in tandem with the Gregorian calendar in this age of globalization? When an imperial era moves on to the next, it must come into people's consciousness that an "old era" has come to an end, and they enter a "new era." This consciousness itself may have some significance worth exploring. With this idea in mind, I make temporal references in terms of the Japanese calendar where it bears certain significance to that consciousness.

Preface

In general, economists take an objective approach to issues, and ideas are verified through data-based analyses. This attitude does not change when they write for general readers: they place themselves outside the object about which they try to give objective and clear accounts. I, for one, have always assumed this manner when I write research papers, removing subjectivity as much as possible to represent a third-person perspective. However, this book is completely different in style. The topics are presented in such a way that various phenomena familiar in our day-to-day contexts are discussed with reference to recent economic study findings. My personal experiences feature in places, too. I did my best to make the content and its presentation provide a glimpse of the humanity in economic thinking, or in other words, the world of *giri ninjo*. Technical terms and jargon are kept to a minimum in order to make the book relevant to readers. I hope it reaches the hands of many people who think economics is rocket science.

Fukuoka, Japan   Eiji Yamamura

Contents

1	**Why Are Koshien High School Baseball Games All Televised?**	1
	Why Do People Watch Live Professional Baseball Games?	4
	Why Did "Tiger Mask" Send Gifts?	6
	What Makes Strong Sumo Wrestlers Stand Apart?	8
	Why Were Mozart, Beethoven, and Liszt Able to Produce Excellent Music?	9
	Can Music Change people's Behavior?	12
2	**Do Mathematical Theories Have National Characteristics?**	17
	How Does the Assimilation of Immigrants Affect the Economy?	18
	Will *Bon Odori* Dance Disappear Amid Globalization?: Ethnic Japanese in Sao Paulo and Jews in New York	21
	The Global Contribution of a Prizefighter in the Showa Era	24
	Why Do Diplomats in New York Park Illegally?	27
	What Good Would It Do if Japanese Anime Was Diffused Across the World?	28
	What Was It in "Oshin" that Won the Hearts and Minds of People Overseas?	31
	Do Children's Values Reflect Their Parents' Values?	35
	What Changes if Fukuzawa Yukichi is Shown on a 10,000-Yen Bill?	38
3	**Why Is It a Secret to Successful Business Management That the Business Owner Treats Job-Seekers to Gourmet Food?**	43
	How Is the French Mentality Relevant to the Arrest of Carlos Ghosn?	47
	What Does Adam Smith Have in Common with an Old Lollipop Man?	50
	What Comes Out from Mixing the Rich and the Poor?	52
	What Can We Learn from the Life of Kazuo Ishiguro About Government Finance?	54
	Municipalities That Fared Well in the Tax-Deductible Donation Scheme by Not Offering Thank-You Gifts	58

	How Can Takarasiennes Always Maintain Their Modesty, Fairness, and Graceful Beauty?—The Reason for the Unwaning Popularity of the Takarazuka Revue Company	62
	How Does Ninjo (Human Sentiments) Enrich the Market Economy?	63
4	**What Will Become of Pupils in a Class with a Female Teacher?**	69
	Women: Are They Born as Women or Do They Become Women?	71
	Women and Men, What Are the Differences?	73
	Are Women Born Non-Competitive or Do They Become Non-Competitive?	76
	Are Women Born to Dislike Math, or Do They Grow to Dislike It?	80
	Equal Employment Opportunities for Men and Women, How Does It Affect the Difference in Height Between a Husband and a Wife?	83
5	**The Reason Why Working Husband and Housekeeping Wife Should Quarrel**	87
	Why Do People Seek Marriage?	91
	What Comes to the Minds of Smokers at the Sight of Their Children?	94
	Having a Working Mother, Does It Determine a Man's Choice of a Woman He Marries?	97
	Does an Arrival of a Daughter Change Her Father's World View?	99
	What Changes Do Grandchildren Engender in Their Grandparents?	101
6	**What Came Out of the Spread of COVID-19?**	105
	Effects of School Closure on Parents' Working Styles	105
	"The Life" of Haruma Miura: "Economics of Duty and Sentiment" Personified	108
	The Postponement of the 2020 Olympic Games and Ninjo the Humanity	112
	Life and Money, Which Is More Important?	116
	The Coronavirus Pandemic and Healthcare Workers' Mental States	118
7	**Concluding Chapter How Can Community Be Rational?**	123
Epilogue		127
References		131

About the Author

Eiji Yamamura is professor of economics at Seinan-Gakuin University, in Fukuoka, Japan. He earned his B.A. and M.A. from Waseda University and a Ph.D. from Tokyo Metropolitan University in 1995, 1999, and 2004, respectively. He has been the executive director of the Association of Behavioral Economics and Finance since 2021. His research topics are behavioral economics, sports economics, income distribution, and household behavior. He has published over 100 papers in peer-reviewed journals including *Regional Studies, Papers in Regional Science, Review of Economics and Statistics, Journal of Economic Behavior and Organization, Journal of Population Economics, Journal of Economic Geography, European Journal of Political Economy, Review of World Economics, Review of International Economics, Economics of Education Review, Public Choice, Economics of Governance, Southern Economic Journal, Review of Economics of the Household, Kyklos, Journal of Cultural Economics, Journal of Sports Economics, Social Science and Medicine, Sustainability*, and the *Journal of the Japanese and International Economies*.

He is also artist, and his tableau *Madoi Bi* ('A Day of Reflection') is on the cover of this book.

Chapter 1
Why Are Koshien High School Baseball Games All Televised?

The ceiling fan was rotating in this cheap lodging house as I lay down on a bed feeling heavy as lead. I had a splitting headache. Locals were flirting and quarreling at the adjacent outdoor bar. In the fall of 1993, I was in Accra, the capital of Ghana in West Africa. I was a poor backpacker traveling around the world for one year. During the trip, I contracted malaria. Before I entered Ghana, I had travelled overland across the French-speaking countries of West Africa. I used local public transportation and sometimes stayed in private homes. Prices were generally high in the French-speaking countries. When I could not buy bottled water, I drank tap water. However, prices were lower in Ghana, an English-speaking nation. Accra is a major city with various amenities. The embassy is also there. I developed malaria on the day I arrived in Accra probably because I had let my guard down.

There I was, in this cheap lodging house, fighting the disease with the medication I received from the hospital. I was struggling with a severe headache, a side effect of the medication. For days, I had difficulty moving; even going to the restroom only three meters away was a struggle. Phil Collins' "Another Day in Paradise" was blaring day after day, over and over, from the bar. I was in a daze and could not understand the lyric. But it resonated in my heart for some reason. I checked the song afterward. It means something like this: It is freezing on the street, and a woman has nowhere to sleep; a man passing by ignores her plea for help; you and me live in a paradise, so we should reach out for those who are less fortunate.

My imagination ran wild. Perhaps I could never go back to Japan. What am I doing in a place like this? Why did I end up being here to begin with? As I stared at the ceiling fan, I was thinking about the last meal I would have before I die. I would have a simple bowl of miso ramen with bean sprouts and pork. I hail from Sapporo. So, this is my soul food. I longed for home. I wanted to go back to Hokkaido, to Sapporo. I fell asleep as I daydreamed.

I had not watched high school baseball for years. Many people seem to think that university professors have lots of free time on their hands once their classes finish. But the fact of the matter is that professors nowadays focus on their research during school breaks, although I do not have much information about what they used to do in the past. I would wake up early in the morning during the summer because I could not stand the heat of Fukuoka, my current home. I would frantically work on my academic paper all day since early in the morning. I would expend all my energy and become completely drained by evening. That was my summer "vacation." Teams that won Koshien games were usually from big cities in Kanto or Kansai. If not, they were from areas with warm weather. There was a vast difference in skills among teams depending on where they were based. I was slightly interested in the performance of teams from Hokkaido, where I was raised. I was able to predict the outcome before they play, though. At best, they could win twice if they were lucky. I was still a novice researcher, and I did not have the luxury to sit back and watch high school baseball all day. One day, while I was spending my summer as usual, I learned over the Internet that a team from Hokkaido was winning. Unfortunately, the team was going up against Yokohama High School, the alma mater of a famous pitcher Daisuke Matsuzaka. The chances were very high that the Hokkaido team would lose by a wide margin. I did not watch the game because I knew what the outcome would be. I learned the result that evening. As I had expected, the game between Yokohama High School and Komazawa University Tomakomai High School ended in a landslide—6 to 1. Nevertheless, I checked the result once again because I had a strange feeling that something was not right. As it turned out, the winner was Komazawa University Tomakomai High School. I checked the result once more thinking that it might be a mistake. However, it was not a mistake; the winner was indeed Komazawa University Tomakomai High School. Feeling that something unusual was about to happen, I kept an eye on the team's next matchup. I checked the game whenever I took a break. The team won again. Thus, the team, for some reason or another, made it to the final. For the final, the team would play with Saibi High School, which had won the spring Koshien tournament and had its sights on a second straight victory in the summer. I watched the game at home from start to finish. My hometown team won. I added Koshien to my research. That was the summer of 2004.

Every year, the professional baseball team Hanshin Tigers go on a long tour known as the "death road" over the *obon* summer holiday period. The Tigers leave their home base for about three weeks and play in various locations throughout Japan as a visiting team. The Hanshin Tigers, one of the most popular professional baseball teams, must leave the stadium because high school students need it. During that period, the Koshien Stadium is occupied all day by high school students as a site for the National High School Baseball Championship (hereinafter "Summer Koshien"). Summer Koshien games—from the first game to the final—are all televised live nationwide on NHK. Even if one lives in Fukuoka, one can watch the initial games between teams from different prefectures. In contrast, only a few of the professional baseball games are televised. Thus, high school students, who are amateurs, are definitely more privileged. People seem to prefer amateur teams with lower skills to professional clubs with the best athletic skills in the nation. This is an extremely strange phenomenon. In order to explain this situation, it is necessary to find out who watch Koshien ballgames.

1 Why Are Koshien High School Baseball Games All Televised? 3

I used the data obtained from a survey of about 9,000 people to examine the effects of Summer Koshien.[1] The survey, which targeted respondents in various locations across Japan, was taken immediately after a Summer Koshien tournament. The data include the prefectures in which the respondents lived at the time of the survey and the prefectures in which they lived when they were around 15 years old. In addition, there is publicly available information regarding the number of games won each year by the teams that represent each prefecture. These data can be used to find out where the respondents lived in the year that the survey was taken and the number of games won by the representative teams of the prefectures where the respondents lived when they were 15 years old. Furthermore, the survey asked the participants about how happy they felt at the time of the survey. In this way, the respondents' level of happiness can be numerically expressed based on five variables from 1 (very unhappy) to 5 (very happy). The above data were used to examine the following:

(1) The effect that a victory of the team representing the location where the respondents currently live may have on their happiness.
(2) The effect that a victory of the team representing the respondents' hometown may have on their happiness.[2] This study, in order to compare people's attachment to their present location and their attachment to their hometown, only targeted people who lived in a different location at the time of the survey from where they lived when they were 15 years old.

The results of the statistical analysis are as follows:

(Result 1) A victory of the team representing the area where people currently live will raise their happiness just as much as a victory of the team representing their hometown.

This effect may differ within the same prefecture depending on whether the respondents live in urban areas or outside major cities. The data include information regarding the population of the areas where the respondents currently live. Using this information, residents in major cities and those outside were examined separately. The results are as follows:

(Result 2) A victory of the team representing the location where people currently live and a victory of the team representing their hometown will both increase their happiness. However, the effect is stronger if the winning

---

[1] Yamamura (2017) uses data from the Japanese General Social Surveys (JGSS). JGSS is a project undertaken by the JGSS Research Center of the Osaka University of Commerce (Joint Usage/Research Center for Japanese General Social Surveys Accredited by the Minister of Education, Culture, Sports, Science and Technology) in collaboration with the Institute of Social Science at the University of Tokyo. JGSS 2000–2008 is designated as an "academic frontier promotion base," while JGSS 2010–2012 receives support from the joint research base promotion project and from the Osaka University of Commerce.

[2] The data also include information on the respondents' income, work, and marital status. A statistical analysis using such information allows for a comparison among people from different income levels by hypothesizing that they have the same level of income. Through this method, the effects of victory that are not influenced by any other factors can be extracted and used for comparison.

team is from their hometown. On the other hand, a victory of neither team affects the happiness of people who do not live in major cities.

Major cities offer a variety of commercial products, providing residents with all kinds of options. These cities may be convenient and comfortable, but people's connection with their hometown tends to become more tenuous. People who live in a lonesome and solitary urban environment may find comfort in their hometown. Even so, the meaning of "hometown" may differ depending on whether people live far away or nearby. For example, a comparison could be made between Tokyo residents who are from Kanagawa and Tokyo residents who are from Hokkaido or Fukuoka. Japan currently has a highly developed transportation system. However, geographical distance affects psychological distance. People's connection to their hometown becomes tenuous in proportion to their physical distance from their hometown. For this reason, various events related to their hometown resonate in their hearts. This examination has yielded the following:

(Result 3) The effect of a hometown team's victory on people's happiness will increase in proportion to the distance between people and their hometown.

People who enjoy Koshien games are residents of cities a long distance away from their hometown. In the Showa era, many people migrated from regional districts to major cities seeking work. NHK, the public broadcaster, airs amateur baseball as a public service for these people. Before each game, NHK almost always shows footage featuring the culture and industry of the areas represented by the teams. City dwellers who come from regional areas watch such footage, recall their childhood, and long for their hometown. One such city dweller is myself as of this writing in 2019.

Why Do People Watch Live Professional Baseball Games?

In baseball, probable starting pitchers are announced in advance. The practice of announcing probable starting pitchers was initially adopted by the Pacific League.[3] In the Showa era, it was often said that the Central League had popularity whereas the Pacific League had skills. In the Central League, an overwhelming number of people filled the stadium whenever the Yomiuri Giants played. The Pacific League put up a good fight with the Central League in the Japan Series and All-Star Series. However, in terms of popularity, the Pacific League was no match for the Central League. Meanwhile, J-League, a professional soccer league, was established in the Heisei era. J-League teams adopted a European approach of staying close to the local community. Baseball, which had been monopolizing the nation's professional sports, began to face competition as a result. The Central League continued to have avid fans, but the Pacific League was on the brink of extinction. Kintetsu Railway in

---

[3] This practice was adopted by the Central League in 2012.

2004 withdrew from baseball. Thus, the Pacific League was under strong pressure to boost its popularity.

I conducted an analysis regarding the demand for professional baseball games by focusing on the fact that the practice of announcing probable starting pitchers was adopted only by the Pacific League at that time.[4] People decide whether to go see a baseball game based on information regarding the game. For example, many fans show a great deal of interest in a game that could determine their team's final victory. Such games are high in demand. It is difficult to acquire a ticket to such games. Data such as team rankings are disclosed to the public by both the Central League and the Pacific League. The practice of announcing probable starting pitchers means that the public also has access to information on these pitchers. In baseball, all players are almost always fixed for each game, except for pitchers. Pitchers have a far greater impact on the outcome of the game than other players. Thus, the pitching position is significant in predicting the outcome. If the starting pitcher is highly capable, there is a greater probability that the team will win. The team will attract more visitors as a result. Among starting pitchers who are equally capable, those who are popular attract more visitors. Then, is it possible to separate pitchers' capabilities from their popularity in conducting an analysis? This can be accomplished by combining the location where a game is played and the starting pitcher's hometown. If a game is held in the starting pitcher's hometown, the pitcher would return home as a hero. This is a case of a hometown boy grows up and makes it big. Many local fans would come to root for their hero. They would be even more excited if their hero is the starting pitcher for the hometown team.

It was not until 2005 when the exact number of visitors began to be announced for each professional baseball game. I collected data for each game from 2005 to 2007. The data include the locations where games were played, annual salaries of the starting pitchers for the hometown team and the visiting team, the starting pitchers' home prefectures, and the cumulative winning percentage of the hometown team and the visiting team during the season up to the game in question. The results of the statistical analysis were exactly what I had expected. In the Pacific League, the higher the annual salary of the starting pitcher, the higher the number of visitors. This effect is three times as great for the starting pitcher of the hometown team as for the starting pitcher of the visiting team. The effect of annual salaries becomes greater if the starting pitchers play in their hometown. The analysis clearly demonstrates that more people show up and root for star players if they hail from their hometown. On the other hand, in the Central League, the starting pitchers' annual salaries or hometown do not affect the number of visitors. This was also what I had expected.

Boys growing up playing baseball do not necessarily become professional players even if they are highly talented or if they work extremely hard. Even if they manage to become pros, only a handful of them get to play in actual games. Therefore, people are proud of a neighborhood boy who succeeds. They come and root for the boy when a game is on. Professional players interact with fans in various events when they are not playing. This is probably a token of their gratitude.

---

[4] Yamamura (2011a).

Why Did "Tiger Mask" Send Gifts?

On Christmas Day in 2010, 10 *randoseru* school backpacks were donated to a child guidance center in the Kanto region. They were sent under the fictitious name of "Naoto Date." This was followed by similar incidents in which many backpacks were donated to orphanages throughout Japan. The series of incidents came to be known as the "Tiger Mask phenomenon."

Tiger Mask, a television anime that was hugely popular in the Showa era, features a professional wrestler wearing a tiger mask. The anime led to the emergence of a real-life professional wrestler, Satoru Sayama, who wore a mask similar to Tiger Mask and created a wrestling boom in Japan. The following is an overview of the cartoon: Naoto Date, who grew up in an orphanage, often visits his home orphanage to encourage children. One day, he takes the children to a local eatery. He tells them that this is a special place where the orphanage children can eat whatever they want without paying. Date, as he leaves the eatery, secretly gives money to the owner and asks him to serve the children whatever they want when they come. The children do not know what this caring elderly brother does for a living. The viewers are the only ones that know that Naoto Date is Tiger Mask, the children's hero. This is a heartwarming story about *giri ninjo*, or a sense of dutiful commitment and empathetic sentiment—what makes us humane.

Tiger Mask is a hero for *shinjinrui* (the new breed of humans), a generation that came of age in the late 1970s. The backpacks provided the recipients with tangible benefits. Their happiness increased as a result. This effect would be the same regardless of who gave the gifts. Then, what difference does it make if the giver is "Tiger Mask"? Tiger Mask is a children's hero. This hero extends a helping hand to children. Therefore, the children, aside from any tangible benefits, will also get a psychological boost. Then, why did the giver ("Tiger Mask") identify himself (or herself) as "Naoto Date," instead of remaining anonymous? After all, if the sender simply wanted to have a feeling of self-satisfaction, remaining anonymous would work just fine. The reason probably has to do with a greater feeling of happiness that the giver would experience by seeing the children become happier. Heroes do not have to be fictitious characters. Keisuke Honda, a world-famous soccer player, launched a business to help people achieve their dream. "This is nothing special. I am just one of those famous and influential people starting a business to help others," he is quoted as saying. "Powerful people should fulfill their responsibility and make sacrifices," Honda says, adding that he wants to see a world where nobody would have to give up a dream because of economic reasons.[5]

In recent years, behavioral economics, which incorporates psychological aspects of human behavior into economics, has been drawing attention. One of the major themes of behavioral economics relates to altruism. I examined how altruism functions by analyzing how people make donations.[6] Among high-income earners, those

---

[5] *"Tsuyoiyatsu no sekinin mattou: honda hinkon to tatakau"* (Fulfilling the obligation of the powerful: Honda fights poverty), *The Nihon Keizai Shimbun*, April 16, 2019. Sports Section, Page 33.

[6] Yamamura (2012 d).

who believe that the disparities between the rich and the poor should be narrowed tend to make larger donations. This is particularly true when it comes to the activities of *chonaikai* neighborhood associations. However, this tendency has not been observed among middle-income and low-income people. This may mean that high-income earners provide more donations as they strengthen their camaraderie with those who earn less. People probably feel motivated to give when they observe that their friends are worse off than they are. In French, there is an expression *noblesse oblige*. This expression means that those who hold a high social status have an obligation to help others and make sacrifices. My studies suggest that there is a similar concept in Japan.[7] Before the advent of behavioral economics, economists had traditionally assumed that humans would act only in pursuit of their own self-interest. According to this view, even though people may appear to act for the benefit of others, they, in fact, do so in order to receive something in return. Take, for example, the Japanese expression *nasakewa hito no tamenarazu* (an act of mercy is not for the sake of others). This expression means that those who provide mercy will eventually get rewarded. Thus, this is not essentially altruistic. If someone has a close relationship with people who are less wealthy, he or she may be able to avoid any potential conflict by providing help. Such an attitude is clearly different from altruism, which seeks to benefit others without expecting anything in return.

The theory of altruism has become so intricate recently that Professor James Andreoni at the University of California, San Diego suggested two concepts regarding this matter. Andreoni suggested that the act of giving, in and of itself, provides the giver with a sense of satisfaction. This effect is called a "warm glow."[8] On the other hand, "pure altruism" is an idea that a person experiences a greater level of happiness not only by the act of giving but also seeing others increase their happiness through his or her giving. It is extremely difficult to discern whether a donation is motived by a desire to receive something in return, driven by a self-serving desire to experience a warm glow, or a result of pure altruism. In recent years, certain empirical methods have been incorporated into economics, with the result that it may soon become possible to discern the motive behind giving.

Nevertheless, in the world outside television, it is still difficult to discern what is going on in people's minds as they give donations. The Tiger Mask phenomenon was a rare occurrence in which all the necessary conditions were in place to create an ideal lab environment. First, the name "Naoto Date" is a pseudonym denoting "Tiger Mask." "Naoto Date" will receive nothing in return by giving. In this sense, it may appear as though this is not much different from an anonymous donation. However, it is different in that the children who receive the gift have a greater level of happiness. "Naoto Date" probably had a mental image of happy children and acted to make this a reality. Thus, the use of the name "Naoto Date" indicates that this was an act of pure altruism.

---

[7] In the U.S., immigrants from Mexico turn to associations of their compatriots to seek help in finding work, place to stay, etc. These associations, led by successful immigrants, prioritize support to women, the elderly, and less-educated people (Munshi 2003).

[8] Andreoni (1989, 1990).

What Makes Strong Sumo Wrestlers Stand Apart?

Among sumo wrestlers who made their debut in the Showa era following World War II, only 22 became *yokozuna* (grand champions). Of those, six were from Hokkaido. These were Taiho, Kitanofuji, Kitanoumi, Chiyonofuji, Onokuni, and Hokutoumi. Five of them were from Aomori, the northern tip of the main island. These were Wakanohana, Tochinoumi, Takanosato, Wakanohana, and Asahifuji. This means that half of the *yokozuna* were either from Hokkaido or Aomori. People from northern Japan become strong sumo wrestlers because they train their leg muscles by walking in the snow. This is what people in Hokkaido (my parents) would say when analyzing the performance of Hokkaido sumo wrestlers. This explanation shall be called the "natural-environment training hypothesis." However, the 22 *yokozuna* do not include anyone from Niigata, which has more snow than Hokkaido. For this reason, the natural-environment training hypothesis is not tenable. Then, how else can we explain the uneven distribution of their home prefecture?

I examined the characteristics of sumo wrestlers' hometowns. Young people in regional districts migrate to Tokyo, home to many sumo stables, to become sumo wrestlers. Unless they are from Tokyo, they must leave their hometown. They join a stable, live with other wrestlers, cook *chankonabe* stew, train their bodies, and hone their skills. Such migrants are not limited to would-be sumo wrestlers. During the period of rapid economic growth, many people who grew up in poor farming households in rural areas migrated as a group to major cities to find work. They migrated from rural areas dominated by the primary industry to urban areas with the secondary and tertiary industries. Young people who migrated from rural districts to join sumo stables in Tokyo and began to live in an urban setting may have at times felt lonely and forlorn and become homesick. However, those who would not be able to find work in their hometown, or those from areas so far away that they could not easily return, were not even able to easily escape Tokyo. According to an article in the *Nihon Keizai* newspaper, Kitanoumi joined the Mihogaseki stable, a poor stable at the time. There, he was presented with the stablemaster's old shoes and red wool socks hand-knit by the stablemaster's wife. He decided to join the stable, thinking to himself that "I will become a disciple of the grandma who gave me the socks."[9] After moving to Tokyo at age 13, he would attend Tokyo's Ryogoku Junior High School while practicing sumo. Now that he entered the world of sumo, he had no other choice but to become a full-fledged wrestler, achieve strong performance, and succeed. Such an attitude may motivate novice wrestlers to focus on sumo and build a strong track record.

Only a handful of sumo wrestlers can reach the status of *yokozuna*. Thus, a sample from a brief period in the postwar era may not provide sufficient data to explain the strength of wrestlers from northern Japan. What is needed, in order to find a general principle, are long-term data on all sumo wrestlers. For this reason, I collected the lifetime performance record and the home prefectures of all sumo wrestlers who

---

[9] "*Nikurashiihodo tsuyokkata*" (Strong enough to generate a feeling of hatred), *The Nihon Keizai Shimbun*, November 21, 2015. Page 43.

made their debut from the Meiji era until 1964, when the Tokyo Olympics were held for the first time. These data were combined with data on the population density of the wrestlers' home prefectures, and these prefectures' distance from Tokyo to create proprietary data for this study. The following is a hypothesis established for conducting this analysis: The longer the period between debut and retirement, the more persistent the wrestler; wrestlers advance in rank as they improve their performance, from *makuuchi* (top division) to *komusubi* (sub-junior champion) to *sekiwake* (junior champion) to *ozeki* (champion) to *yokozuna* (grand champion); the higher the rank that a wrestler achieves during his career, the higher the performance. In economics, it is held that the higher the population density, the more active the economic activity and the more developed the economy. This means that finding a job is easier in an area with a high population density. When Japan did not have a highly developed transportation system, it was extremely costly to move from one location to another, unlike now. My statistical analysis has resulted in the following findings:

(Result 1) The harder the job search in a wrestler's hometown, the longer the career and the higher the rank of the wrestler.
(Result 2) The longer the distance between a wrestler's hometown and Tokyo, the longer the career and the higher the rank of the wrestler.

All this took place before Japan joined the ranks of major industrialized nations. Country boys fought their battle alongside the grown-ups in a big city. They would visit their hometown only if they were to succeed in their sumo career and gain social recognition. Until then, they could not return. The more determined they were, the more successful they became in their sumo career.

Why Were Mozart, Beethoven, and Liszt Able to Produce Excellent Music?

The studies of sumo wrestlers suggest that the location and the environment in which people were raised may affect their motivation and help them achieve success in their career. This may indicate the importance of one's life circumstances before launching a career. However, people encounter all kinds of unexpected occurrences once they actually start working. Personal life events, even if they do not appear to be directly related to work, influence people's physical and mental conditions. Such events may even influence their professional life. There is a saying in Japan that one should experience hardship even if it has to be purchased. This may sound foolish from the standpoint of economics. In the market economy, a transaction is carried out when the buyer determines that a certain good would produce greater value than the price paid. Normally, hardship does not produce satisfaction. Thus, people do not purchase hardship. However, an unexpected conclusion could be reached if one takes a different perspective. Hardship is a type of training. In a competitive society, there are always losers. When people lose, they wonder why they lost. They will try to come up with a measure to win next time. At the same time, they will also be able to relate to the sadness of others who have lost. Such an experience would help them build character, rather than simply improve their technique. A research group led by Fumio Ohtake at Osaka University found that children who experienced competition in elementary schools were aided by that experience in their character formation as adults.[10] Thus, experiencing hardship may help people improve their character and capabilities, with the result that they may turn into highly competent professionals. If this is the case, the saying that one should experience hardship even if it has to be purchased may have a common sensical implication that one should actively make investments to improve their professional capabilities. There is a mountain of studies in the field of economics that examined this issue.

In reality, sometimes a disaster falls on people whether they like it or not. Some people live a life of hardship. The movie *Amadeus*, released in 1984, is a work that depicts the life of Mozart. In the film, Mozart is highly energetic and prone to act in an eccentric fashion. He bursts into laughter whenever and wherever he feels like it. Seated behind a piano, Mozart produces beautiful music quickly, on the fly; music comes naturally to this genius like breathing. However, Mozart does not read the situation around him, and for this reason, he does not receive the recognition that he deserves from society. Ironically, it is Mozart's nemesis that understands his abilities the most, and out of sheer jealousy, this archenemy seeks to take his life. In this semi-fictional film, Mozart's raw humanness comes through as he is tossed around by fate and leaves an indelible impression on the viewer. Accidental occurrences in life may cause various emotions in people and influence their creativity. Karol J. Borowiecki, a cultural economist at the University of Southern Denmark, examined the relationship of the life of Mozart, Beethoven, and Liszt with the quality of their works.[11]

Borowiecki first set out to express the composers' emotions in numerical terms. Major events in their life, and at what age they experienced such events, can be found in their critical biographies. These events include marriage, love affairs, the death of parents, and separation. Still, biographies alone may not provide enough information for understanding their inner thoughts. Fortunately, about 1,400 letters they wrote still exist today, and they are all preserved digitally. The composers' psychological conditions at various times can be numerically expressed by analyzing the content, phrases, and expressions of these letters with the use of artificial intelligence (AI). Borowiecki writes that there is a consistent relationship between major life events of the composers and their psychological conditions. For example, deaths or divorce put them in a negative psychological condition.

At the same time, the quality and the quantity of the composers' works were also numerically expressed. The quantity can be easily expressed in numerical terms based

---

[10] People who had attended elementary schools that discouraged competition, as adults, tended to be less trusting of others, less willing to cooperate with others, and less likely to reciprocate others' kindness (Ito et al. 2021).

[11] These composers were chosen for two reasons. (1) They can be easily compared with one another because they were contemporaries. (2) There are extant letters they wrote from the time they began to compose music until they ended their career (Borowiecki 2017).

on the number and the length of their works. The quality was expressed in numerical terms based on how their works are currently evaluated. Borowiecki used the latest technology to build a proprietary database based on a vast amount of historical documents related to music. A statistical analysis of these data has revealed that famous music was created when the composers were in a negative psychological condition. They created outstanding music as they toiled amid agony and despair. This is true even for a genius like Mozart. It has been scientifically proven that suffering can improve artists' creativity.

As exhibited in Fig. 1.1, I remember the portrait of Beethoven hung in the music room of my elementary school and junior high school. I was actually scared by the ferocious expression on his face. It is well known that Beethoven developed hearing difficulties when he was still young and eventually became deaf. I can picture Beethoven tearing out his hair in frustration while composing music. He left us music that stirs our soul. The genius Beethoven carried the cross of suffering and gave birth to classical music that went down in history.

Perhaps these great composers are communicating to people in the present age that one should experience hardship even if it has to be purchased.

Fig. 1.1 A portrait of Beethoven. *Source* https://publicdomainq.net/joseph-karl-stieler-0000383/

Can Music Change people's Behavior?

Music is played everywhere in Japanese towns. Why is music even necessary when it has nothing to do with the merchandise being offered? Heavy metal music was blaring at an all-you-can-eat joint that I stopped by for lunch in Tokyo's Shibuya district. I thought perhaps it had something to do with the culture of the district, but the customer sitting next to me grumbled that the music made him lose his appetite. Come to think of it, all-you-can-eat restaurants will be able to reduce their expenses and increase profits if customers do not eat. Even so, people who visit this "all-you-can-eat" place would probably never come back, and the eatery would acquire a bad reputation. As it turned out, this establishment operated as an *izakaya* pub at night, its mainstay business. It provided lunch on the side to put its daytime hours to effective use. Therefore, any losses from the lunchtime mismanagement may not have been so huge. It may be that this establishment was simply trying out various different formats without expecting much to begin with.

Some types of music reduce people's appetite. However, there are also types of music that make people feel good. Paul J. Zak, an expert on *ninjo* (human empathy) economics, recounts an experience "As I listened to the music, my entire body pulsed with an overwhelming sense of love and belonging and peace. Tears streaming down my face, I felt a revelatory sense of connection with the entire universe…I was floating in a boundless see of love, with wave of kindness and connection washing over me".[12] Zak, based on his personal experience, decided to examine the effects that music and dance may have on human psyche. He invited research participants to a social dance club and asked them to dance. He collected blood samples from the participants before and after the dance and examined the content. Under his rules, participants form pairs and dance to the music. They change partners from time to time so that each participant can form pairs with all the other participants. This is how he examined the way in which dance, music, and human interaction may influence people's physical and mental conditions. In particular, he focused on a substance called oxytocin. Oxytocin, which exists in large amounts in women's bodies, rises when a mother breast-feeds her baby. When the level of oxytocin rises, the person experiences the feeling of love and togetherness and becomes happier. Oxytocin is the hormone of love and affection.[13] Men typically have less oxytocin than women. However, the level of oxytocin rises in men's bodies when they have an experience like Zak's music encounter. This experiment demonstrated that the participants had

---

[12] Zak (2012:132). "*Ninjo* (human empathy) economics" is the name that I (Yamamura) assigned to a certain field of economics.

[13] Karori Matsumoto, who won gold medal in Judo in the 2012 London Olympics, was known as "*yaju*" (wild animal) for her fighting spirit. She subsequently got married, gave birth in 2017, and announced her retirement in February 2019. She said that she would retire because her priority was her child, not judo. The "wild animal" probably had more oxytocin in her body after she gave birth. Matsumoto had fierce expressions on her face as a judo practitioner. However, when she spoke at a news conference to announce her retirement, her facial expressions looked so gentle that she reminded me of the Virgin Mary.

more oxytocin in their bodies after they danced. Music and dance make people feel happy.

The movie *Bohemian Rhapsody* was released toward the end of 2018. The film features Freddie Mercury, the lead singer of the rock band Queen. I have watched *Bohemian Rhapsody* in a movie theater twice as of this writing in January 2019. When I watch the film for a third time, I will do so, again, in a movie theater. I have heard that people, once they watch the movie, will get hooked and watch it multiple times in a movie theater, just like myself. Thus, the movie has become something of a social phenomenon. In an age when various media platforms are readily available, there seem to be very few movies that would make it worthwhile for people to actually visit a movie theater. Even if they do visit a theater, they may not find it worthwhile to go back and watch the same movie multiple times. This can be explained by one of the fundamental principles of economics discussed in an introductory textbook for college freshmen. People will receive great satisfaction by watching a movie for the first time. However, they will experience less satisfaction the second time. When they watch the movie for the third time, their satisfaction declines even further. Those who are interested in a movie will watch it immediately after the release. For this reason, the demand is highest immediately after the release, and it gradually declines afterward. Existing data also suggest that the demand for most movies follows this textbook pattern. However, as an economist, I see an anomaly. I was moved by *Bohemian Rhapsody* the second time more than the first time. The more I learned about Freddie's songs and his life, the more moved I became. There is something about this movie that appeals to human empathy and makes people want to share that experience with someone. That someone also visits the theater, becomes hooked, and tells someone else about it. The demand for *Bohemian Rhapsody* rises because of such a mechanism, the textbook economic principles notwithstanding.

Freddie's sorrow and agony reverberate in my heart as he crafts beautiful yet ingenious music with fellow band members. Viewers are captivated by Freddie's appearance and powerful singing voice in the final scene, where he belts out at Live Aid. People who have experienced Queen's live performance are now probably about 70 years as oldest. Their children may be about 40, and grandchildren in their teens attending junior high or high schools. In the theater, various people—men and women, young and old, couples, parents and children—shed tears as Freddie sings. The bond of empathy expands beyond age, gender, and nationality.

Oxytocin not only enhances people's contentment and happiness but also prompts them to share such feelings with others. Those who have watched *Bohemian Rhapsody* will try to convey its appeal and share how they were inspired by Queen's music, Freddie's singing, and Freddie's life. Queen's songs, such as "Bohemian Rhapsody," are not only heard but also sung along. The ballad segment of *Bohemian Rhapsody* is about a wayward son crying out to his mother and asking her to carry on as if nothing really matters. People who sing with Freddie experience a surge of oxytocin, the love hormone, in their bodies. Zak writes that oxytocin makes people act in a generous and considerate manner even toward complete strangers. In other words, people approach others in an empathetic manner, and they begin to act ethically as a result. Ethical

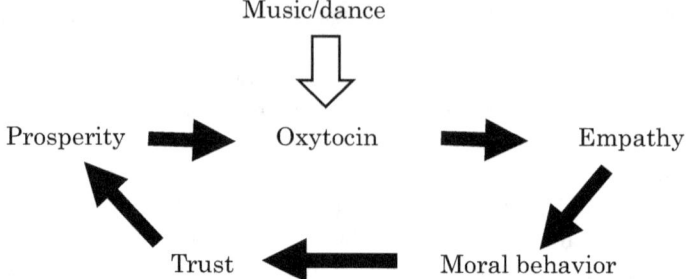

Fig. 1.2 Virtuous cycle

behavior strengthens the trust among people. Trust, which facilitates transactions, is essential for the market economy to function.

One of the challenges of modern economics is to make market transactions trustworthy. Adam Smith writes that individuals who pursue their own interest, through God's "invisible hand," stimulate the market and produce wealth. However, people may sometimes lie in order to pursue their self-interest when God is not watching. If there is a possibility that a person could be deceived, the person may hesitate to carry out a transaction in order to avoid losses. As a result, the market economy ceases to function. Thus, the establishment of trust is important for the functioning of the market economy.

When trust is established, transactions are carried out among people. Wealth is created as a result. When wealth spreads throughout society, people will put more value on the meaning of life or empathy toward others, rather than the pursuit of material gains. The cycle that begins with empathy eventually returns to empathy. Zak calls this mechanism "Virtuous Cycle."[14] Music and dance are catalysts for such a cycle. This mechanism is illustrated in Fig. 1.2.

To my knowledge, there has not been any major experiment conducted to validate the above mechanism. However, there was a case in which a closely related policy was implemented on an experimental basis. The place was Bogota, Colombia, which was feared among backpackers in the 1990s as one of the world's three most dangerous cities.[15] Bogota was so infested with crime that people had to avoid this city unless they wanted to die. There were 4,200 cases of murder in Bogota in 1993 alone. Of course, I stayed away from that dangerous city. In October 1994, several months after I left Latin America, philosophy professor Antanas Mockus became the mayor of Bogota. The city was transformed by the unusual policies that Mockus implemented. The crime rate plummeted, and the city became a beautiful tourist destination. What did Mayor Mockus do? He deployed pantomime performers. They took the place of police officers to handle various traffic violations.[16] They would follow jaywalkers or vehicles that violated traffic rules. They would imitate all the body movements of the

---

[14] Zak (2012:160).

[15] The other two are Lagos, Nigeria, and Kinshasa, Zaire (now Congo).

[16] Zak (2012: Chap 4) Fisman and Miguel (2014: Chap. 4).

traffic violators and make fun of them. People did not want to be mocked. Therefore, the number of traffic accidents and violations declined dramatically. The ratio of pedestrians who obeyed traffic lights rose from 26 to 75%. The use of water declined by 40% after Mayor Mockus took a shower on television and demonstrated how to save water. The mayor acted like a circus clown to elicit empathy. Laughter led to a decline in violence and crime. Thus, pantomiming raised Bogota people's oxytocin and resuscitated the city. Subsequently, Colombia emerged as one of the highest-ranking nations in terms of people's happiness in an OECD survey. The mentality of the people of Bogota has been expressed as follows: The people of Colombia enjoy themselves a lot and laugh a lot … They know how to entertain others. If you enjoy your work, customers will also notice, and they will also become happy. You must be happy and glad.[17] This is very different from introductory economics, which is based on the premise that people find labor painful. What introductory economics fails to consider is the empathy that people feel toward others when they work. "*Ninjo* (human empathy) economics," on the other hand, studies how to raise the level of empathy that people feel toward others while working.

---

[17] Maike van den Boom (2016:239).

Chapter 2
Do Mathematical Theories Have National Characteristics?

"Culture" is an amorphous and ambiguous concept that is difficult to pin down. In economics, the target of analysis is influenced by culture. Economics, even though it is a social science, uses methods similar to those of hard sciences. Still, economics does not provide the clarity or precision that is universally applicable. In contrast, hard sciences are precise and universally applicable. In particular, mathematics is a precise science that is not influenced by language or culture. There is a world of difference between mathematics and other disciplines when it comes to completeness and universality. Thus, many economists revere mathematicians (or so it seems).

I lived in Munich for one year from 2008 for my research. In the same lodging house, there lived a researcher who was almost the same age as myself and who was also originally from Sapporo, Hokkaido. This was Tomohiro Sasamoto, a mathematical physicist, now professor at the Tokyo Institute of Technology.[1] Munich and Sapporo are sister cities, and they also have similar climates. I had the privilege to interact with Sasamoto; after all, we were from the same hometown. One day, I said to him: "The beauty of mathematics is that cultural differences do not matter and that everyone in the world can understand mathematics." Sasamoto immediately responded: "There is certainly such an aspect. However, mathematicians in various countries have different styles that reflect the cultural influences of their nations. In Germany, there is German mathematics. In Britain, there is British mathematics. In France, there is French mathematics. In Japan, there is Japanese mathematics." I was taken aback. According to Sasamoto, mathematics in Germany is hefty and vigorous, while mathematics in Britain is practical with a good balance of theory and application. In France, mathematics is elegant, although there are aspects whose application is unclear. In Japan, mathematics is an accumulation of intuitions and experiences aimed at a level that nobody else could ever attain.

---

[1] Sasamoto received Young Scientist Award in Statistical Physics, an international prize. In Japan, he received Nishinomiya-Yukawa Memorial Prize, Ryogo Kubo Memorial Prize, and the MSJ Analysis Prize. Sasamoto is esteemed internationally, and he influenced Martin Hairer, who received a 2014 Fields Medal. Tokyo Institute of Technology website, accessed January 26, 2019, https://educ.titech.ac.jp/phys/news/2016_09/052670.html

I interpret Sasamoto's remarks to mean that although mathematics is universal, it is also influenced by culture. The national characteristics that come to mind when we think about certain countries are clearly reflected in mathematical formulas. Culture is born of the history of people and the environment in which they were raised. This is reflected in the way in which people use logic. Economics has been creating analytical frameworks for intricate human behavior by identifying the universal human characteristics. Cultural elements are regarded as nothing more than an "error" to be adjusted. However, the more we think about it, the more aware we become that culture cannot simply be ignored. In recent years, economists are beginning to recognize this reality.

What is the significance of the remarks made by the mathematical physicist with whom I share a hometown? I have been asking myself this question for 10 years. This is what I have found so far: Economists would not be able to understand true human behavior if they continue to avoid this question. When they tackle this issue, they would become a tad wiser.

How Does the Assimilation of Immigrants Affect the Economy?

Books were lined up and neatly displayed on the shelf. I chose two that were noticeably thin. These were Franz Kafka's *The Metamorphosis* and Albert Camus' *The Stranger.* In 1981, I just graduated from elementary school and became a junior high school student. I had an urge to read books with lots of small characters—books that adults would read—and learn about a world that I did not know anything about. I stepped into a university bookstore near my home and headed straight toward the *bunkobon* (Japanese-style paperbacks) novel section. Books that are too thick would be difficult to read. So, I was looking for books that would be easier. What I immediately noticed were *The Metamorphosis* and *The Stranger.* Reading an exotic novel would be a perfect way to join grown-ups. After careful consideration, I bought *The Stranger.* I lay down on my bed and opened the book. "Maman died today. Or yesterday maybe, I don't know."

I was perplexed right from the beginning; after all, I was just a seventh grader. Nevertheless, I kept on reading until the very end. The protagonist's action was incomprehensible from start to finish. I thought that the story was rather disturbing, but nothing really stayed in my memory. It was more than a decade later, in the late fall of 1995, when I again got ahold of a copy of *The Stranger.* I returned home after recovering from malaria in West Africa and began to study French at Athénée Français in Tokyo's Ochanomizu district. There, *L'Étranger*, Camus' original work in French, was recommended for beginning students. So, I decided to read it. I chose this book when I was a seventh grader, and again when I was in my mid-20s, not because I was interested in the content but because I thought it would be short and easy. It turned out, however, that the content was not that easy.

In the nineteenth century, a man born in Bordeaux, France settled in Algeria to engage in agriculture. Albert Camus is a great-grandson of this man. The family had been in Algeria for four generations. Unlike other French colonies, Algeria, until its independence in 1962, had a prefecture that was treated in the same way as those of mainland France. Camus was raised in poverty; members of his family, although they were white, could not read or write. *The Stranger,* a story set in Algeria, was written by this author and published in 1942. The protagonist, Meursault, belongs to a low-income stratum of society. His daily life involves interaction with "Arabs." On a certain sun-scorched day, he shoots to death an Arab who comes at him with a sword. The latter half of the story describes Meursault's trial, in which he acts and speaks in an unrepentant manner. He is defiant toward the priest who visits him after the trial. Meursault is a loner who does not submit to anyone and who does not bond with anyone.

The Stranger is set against the backdrop of strife and discord among ethnic groups with different social and cultural norms. Meursault is an extremely poor communicator. He has trouble communicating not only with Arabs but also with almost everyone. The incident would not have occurred had Meursault been sociable and warm-hearted. Then, the novelist would be in trouble because that would not make a good story. This would be a great topic for an economist, though.

In team sports, it is important that members understand, and communicate with, one another. In soccer, one of the most popular sports in the world, communication between the passer and the receiver is important for successful passes. During a game, team members share the same strategy in a variety of situations while passing and receiving as they attack. Take, for example, the mighty FC Barcelona from its past glorious years. Recall how the team performed its splendid attacking passes. All members trusted one another as they collaborated and made many successful passes to confound their opponents—their performance is truly a work of art created by the entire team. The success of FC Barcelona was based on effective communication between team members and the shared team philosophy.

I examined soccer teams representing various countries to study the importance of communication from the standpoint of economics.[2] The strength of various national teams is displayed in the monthly world ranking released by the FIFA. I examined the data from 1993 to 1998 to identify the characteristics of the national teams that went up in ranking. For Japan, playing in the World Cup had been a pipe dream for a long time. However, the Japan national team, which entered the World Cup for the first time in 1998, has been consistently winning the qualifiers ever since. In the 2018 World Cup held in Russia, Japan demonstrated the power of team cohesion by defeating Colombia, the soccer powerhouse. Japan's rapid advancement was due, in large part, to the creation of J-League, a professional soccer league, in 1993. The man instrumental in galvanizing J-League was the legendary Zico (Arthur Antunes Coimbra), who once represented Brazil as a star player. Zico joined Kashima Antlers and contributed to the team's advancement as a player and a coach. Many other players and coaches also jointed J-League from countries known for their soccer

---

[2] Yamamura (2012c).

culture. This is how Japan attained the advanced skills of soccer. The fact that many foreigners have served as coaches for the Japan national team implies that skills brought from overseas had a great impact on the nation's soccer. Such a phenomenon is not limited to soccer. In fact, this is widely recognized as a pattern that developing countries follow in improving their economies.[3] My statistical analysis using the FIFA ranking also confirmed that the introduction of new techniques from other countries would have the effect of helping a nation improve its ranking. The analysis has resulted in the following intriguing findings:

(Result 1)   The more languages spoken in a nation, the weaker the effects of foreign techniques.
(Result 2)   Negative effects of linguistic diversity can be observed in industrialized nations, but not in developing countries.

Result 1 can be interpreted as follows. When various languages are spoken, communication among athletes becomes difficult. For this reason, sharing new techniques will also become difficult. Result 2 means that a high level of communication is not necessary in a country where the technique level is low because the level of new techniques introduced to such a nation is also low. Thus, what is required is for players to simply train their bodies on their own. However, new techniques introduced to a country where the level is already high may require that the strategy and philosophy associated with these techniques be understood and shared. For example, FC Barcelona, which performs the most magnificent passes, has many players trained in an organization affiliated with the team. This is because the team's mission cannot be accomplished unless all members understand and share the underlying philosophy. Japanese players often find it difficult to play in Europe, the center of all the action, even if they have great skills. This is due, in part, to their weak language skills. Hidetoshi Nakata, one of the few Japanese players who succeeded in Europe, was able to freely communicate with other team members thanks to his outstanding language skills. Italy's Serie A, in which Nakata played, is one of the top soccer leagues in the world. Nakata is a hero who led the prestigious Associazione Sportiva Roma to its first victory in 18 years in 2001. For this reason, he still remains vivid in the mind of many people of Rome.[4] The importance of language communication becomes apparent when an organization must meet challenging requirements.

Here, a parallel could be drawn to the world of business. Communication skills are absolutely important in various decision-making processes within a corporation, such as product development and the opening of new sales routes. Soccer players also move from team to team all across the world throughout their career. This, too, is observed among workers in a globalized labor market. Communication abilities are most important regardless of one's country or organization. In a global community, one must communicate with people with various different identities even as one maintains his or her own identity. Sharing a common language as a means of communication will help improve economic efficiency.

---

[3] Hayami (2000).

[4] This is based on an interview with Fabio Sabatini, an economist at Sapienza University of Rome.

A common language emerges with the formation of a market economy in which anyone can participate without being discriminated against. English has become a global language because it is a tool for entering the market. Thus, economists often argue for the usefulness of linguistic assimilation from the viewpoint of efficiency.[5] However, such an argument fails to take into account the role of language in shaping culture and national identity. Language, as an identity marker, deepens thinking, evokes nostalgia, and makes people visualize their future. Language as an identity marker also evokes the sense of obligation and human empathy rooted in a person's culture. This raises a question as to whether a language, as a mere tool, can truly express the sense of obligation and human empathy. As mentioned at the beginning of this chapter, even mathematics, which is supposed to be a universal language, is steeped in culture. Thus, an argument could be made that creative work may require emotions and sensitivities backed by a person's identity.[6] Even as AI plays an increasingly important role, humans still maintain an advantage when it comes to creativity. As Japanese, would we be able to improve our disposition and sensibility, and deepen our thinking, if we use English as a mere tool?

People's geographical movements will result in linguistic diversification. When this takes place, we will all become "strangers" with different linguistic identities. There will emerge a common language as a tool for co-existing with others and a common currency as a medium of exchange in the marketplace. As national borders become less of a barrier amid globalization, English and the U.S. dollar gain wide currency around the world. Here are my questions for people in the distant future: Is English an identity marker common to all mankind? Can "strangers" meet someone with whom they can establish a deep emotional connection?

Will *Bon Odori* Dance Disappear Amid Globalization?: Ethnic Japanese in Sao Paulo and Jews in New York

I remember watching *Kohaku Uta Gassen* (red and white song battle) on New Year's Day 25 years ago. Sachiko Kobayashi puts on gigantic peacock feathers and rises through the air. Those who are watching this video with me are not my family members. They are backpackers sharing the same room with me. I was staying in a cheap lodging house in La Paz, the capital of Bolivia. This was a boardinghouse run by a Japanese owner, and most of the guests were backpackers from Japan. The singing video, taped a year earlier, was one of the rental titles available for the guests. We were watching *Kohaku Uta Gassen* because it is an annual ritual in Japan to watch it on New Year's Eve. However, this was not the only time that I listened to Japanese songs in Latin America. I have an experience of listening to Japanese songs live with many audience members. I was in Liberdade, a Japanese district of Sao Paulo, Brazil, where I visited a community hall for ethnic Japanese people. It

---

[5] Powell (2016, Chap. 4).

[6] Fujiwara (2005).

just so happened that a singing event was being held there. Most people were singing in beautiful Japanese. It was like NHK *Nodo Jiman*, an amateur singing show aired every Sunday noon in Japan. Figure 2.1 shows photos of singers in the show.

A girl who appeared to be an elementary school student was singing "*Ichiendama no tabi garasu*" (the one-yen coin traveling crow). The song seemed to be very

Fig. 2.1 Photograph: I took this photo in 1994 at the entrance of the Japanese community hall, where a singing event was being held among ethnic-Japanese people in Sao Paulo. The photos displayed at the entrance were those of past participants. They have a Japanese appearance, but somehow there is something exotic about them. These women are ethnic-Japanese Brazilians. © Eiji Yamamura

popular in Brazil because five or six children were singing it. It was from *Min-na no uta* (children's songs), brief anime clips aired on NHK Television. The song features a traveling humanoid crow with a head that looks like a huge one-yen coin. Here I was, myself a traveling crow, from Japan. Ethnic Japanese people around me were also descendants of those who traveled all the way from Japan. When they learned that I was Japanese, they smiled and spoke to me in Japanese. They told me that "Marcia," a Japanese-Brazilian singer who made a name for herself in Japan, had taken part in this singing event a few years earlier. In the ethnic-Japanese community, a person's status rises in proportion to his or her Japanese-language skills. While walking the streets of Liberdade, I encountered a strange scene. In front of a secondhand-record shop was a row of *enka* ballad phonograph records from Japan, including those of Saburo Kitajima, Haruo Minami, and Hibari Misora. They all looked young. These were from the mid-1950s to the mid-1960s, before I was born. This was the Japan that I had not experienced before.

Immigrants maintain their own distinct culture in a foreign land. Such a phenomenon is not unique to ethnic-Japanese people. Examining such a phenomenon also falls within the purview of economics. Christianity spread throughout Western Europe and exerted a tremendous impact on the region's culture and history. Christmas is a major event in which people celebrate the birth of Christ. However, I had a very interesting experience in New York, where I visited during the Christmas season in 2004. There was a concert by a reggae musician at a music club in Central Square. This was different from other reggae concerts in that it incorporated Jewish ethnic music. This club was normally packed with many young people. On that particular day, there were all kinds of people—from children to elderly men. Some were shaking hands in a friendly fashion while others were giving one another high fives. Some people showed up in Orthodox Jewish attire, all in black, while others were wearing jeans. At minimum, everyone was wearing a traditional skullcap, except for me. The mesmerizing Jewish reggae lulled me into a world of fantasy. It appeared that a Jewish community festival was being held in this music club in the middle of Manhattan.

Western Europe has been home to a certain number of Jewish people, who have been maintaining their own unique lifestyle and culture for a long time. Their culture and practices include a festival called Hanukkah. It just so happened that the festival takes place in December. Jewish parents give gifts to children during the festival, just as Christian parents do for Christmas. For this reason, Hanukkah is sometimes called the Jewish Christmas. It seems that I was attending a Hanukkah-related gathering in New York.

In the U.S., Jewish people comprise only about 2% of the population. Hanukkah is an extremely important festival for Jewish people in the U.S., although it may not be all that significant in Israel. Suppose that a student who is not particularly eager to study is placed in a classroom where all other students are extremely diligent. Then, this student would probably start working harder. Conversely, if a diligent student is placed in a classroom where other students do not enjoy studying, this student would probably become less diligent. In economics, this phenomenon is explained by "peer effects." In the U.S., the entire nation celebrates Christmas on a grand scale. Thus, peer effects may make Jewish people want to celebrate Christmas just like others. This is especially the case for children who are in their formative years as they see their classmates all geared up for Christmas. Therefore, there is a possibility that their parents, who follow Judaism and seek to maintain their Jewish identity, may also feel compelled to celebrate Hanukkah amid all the Christmas festivities. This may explain why Jewish people in the U.S., where they are in the minority, are more strongly motivated to maintain their tradition than Jewish people in Israel, where they are in the majority. There is an economic analysis that examined the extent to which Jewish people in the U.S. participate in Hanukkah around Christmas.[7] The results are as follows:

(Result 1)   Those who celebrate Hanukkah tend to be parents with small children.
(Result 2)   The smaller the percentage of Jewish households in a given district, the larger the percentage that each Jewish household spends on Hanukkah.

Immigrants practice their tradition not only to enjoy themselves but also to protect their culture from influences of their host nation as they seek to maintain their identity through generations.

When I was staying in La Paz, I went to a music shop and bought a cassette recommended by a clerk. It was *Mi Tierra*, an album by Gloria Estefan, the lead singer for the Miami Sound Machine. She is an immigrant from Cuba raised in Miami. Her English disco tunes were great hits a few years earlier, but this album was entirely in Spanish. "Mi Tierra" in the album *Mi Tierra* is a nostalgic ballad. I listened to "Mi Tierra" in my lodging house. I recalled that I am also a descendant of an immigrant, an immigrant who migrated to Hokkaido.

The Global Contribution of a Prizefighter in the Showa Era

On the table was a magazine on the game of Go. When I flipped through the pages, there was a photo of a portly man past middle age facing a checkerboard. With his hair disheveled, he had two buttons undone but wore a tie. The man might be drunk. Although he appeared exhausted, I could still detect his fighting spirit and fierce determination. He did not have the wasted look of a drunkard. Instead, this was a man full of vitality, like a wild animal on the prowl. There was something scary about him. These headlines jumped out at me: "Hideyuki wins the midnight duel!" and "Improbable victory at the last minute!" The photo was that of a Go champion named Hideyuki Fujisawa. It seemed that he had just defended his title. This was in the mid-1970s, when I was in elementary school.

My father played Go as a hobby. So, we often watched Go lessons and games on NHK TV on Sundays. On television, Fujisawa was a funny and friendly man. He was always joking around even as he gave insightful commentary. This was a completely different person from the individual in the photo, a prizefighter with a killer instinct.

---

[7] Abramitzky et al. (2010).

Hideyuki is a Go legend. Given to drunkenness and gambling, he accumulated a large amount of debt. Although his personal life was in shambles, his power was unparalleled in high-stake games. He continued to defend his titles in many games. In particular, he defended the title of *kisei* (Go Sage) for six games in a row. He was addicted to alcohol, but he would quit cold turkey prior to games. That photo was probably taken immediately after he had defended his title. He staked his life on Go to pay back his debt; the prize money was huge. This was a grown-up who would never appear in a school textbook, but his charm was irresistible. He acquired his formidable skills and abilities at the risk of his life, but passed them on so generously to younger players. This was a big man with a warm heart. Many young players rallied around Hideyuki in a way reminiscent of how the mighty and strong gathered at Mount Liang in the Chinese novel *Water Margin*.

The *Nihon Keizai* newspaper carried an article on January 18, 2019, the final year of the Heisei era, that Nihon Ki-in, the association of Go players, established a program for *eisai* (gifted people) to train young players as the country seeks to catch up with China and South Korea. It was reported that Sumire Nakamura, a nine-year old fourth grader, became the youngest person in the history of Go to become a professional player. Until about two decades ago, Japan was a dominant powerhouse in the world of Go. Nowadays, however, the nation lags far behind China and South Korea. Japanese players have difficulty even winning preliminary games. Many of the world's top Go players are those from China and South Korea between the age of 10 and 20. Among Japanese players, Yuta Iyama, a domestic title holder, may be the only one who could compete head-to-head with them. The new program was established in order to provide special training to children. They would become professional at a young age and equip themselves for global competitions. Nakamura became the youngest professional player under this program.

In economics, a typical growth approach for developing nations is a catch-up model. Under this model, developing countries will play catch-up by imitating, and acquiring technology from, major industrialized nations. This mechanism may explain why China and South Korea surpassed Japan in Go. During the Showa era, China and South Korea, which did not have strong Go techniques, had to learn from Japan. How did they learn Japan's advanced Go techniques? This is where Hideyuki Fujisawa played an important role.[8] Starting in the 1980s, Hideyuki gathered together Japan's best Go players—they were his disciples—and frequently visited China to teach people how to play Go. This led to a significant improvement in the abilities of top Chinese Go players. Some people in Japan were critical that he was carelessly giving away Japan's hard-earned techniques. Hideyuki dismissed such criticism and continued to teach Go in his usual magnanimous way. Many top Chinese players in the previous generation learned from Hideyuki as children. In the best-of-three game that took place in 1999 to mark his retirement, he played with players from Japan, China, and South Korea.[9] Top players in China and South Korea today are "grandchildren" of Hideyuki, who is ultimately responsible for their success. Hideyuki died

---

[8] Fujisawa (2012: 296–299).
[9] *Go World*, July 2010.

in 2009. At the memorial gathering, a top South Korean player said: "I am neither a disciple nor a child, but he loved me more than his disciples or children."

Players who came in contact with Hideyuki Fujisawa may all have felt the same way, regardless of their nationality. Humans could be classified into two types: Dionysian and Apollonian, an idea drawn from the ancient Greek mythology. People with Dionysian traits act according to their passion, while those with Apollonian traits act based on reason. These two opposite poles existed side-by-side in Hideyuki Fujisawa.

Alfred Marshall, the 19th-century economist, spoke of the need for "cool heads but warm hearts." Marshall, who had studied philosophy and taught moral philosophy, eventually began to place a greater emphasis on social concerns and questioned whether opportunities in life should be limited to only a handful of people.[10] Marshall subsequently became an economist and pursued studies that formed the foundation of modern economics. Marshall's "cool heads" probably had to do with economic technology, while "warm hearts" may have been rooted in the moral philosophy that he learned as a young man. Economics has relevance only if these two elements are present. A warm-hearted idealist would end up becoming a mere dreamer unless he or she has solid knowledge about mathematics or statistics. On the other hand, an economist armed with sophisticated tools would become socially irrelevant if he or she does not have a broad perspective and empathy.

There is an economist who cites Hideyuki Fujisawa. Akihiko Matsui, who specializes in game theory, is a nephew of Hideyuki Fujisawa.[11] Matsui, in discussing the books that have influenced him the most, refers to Marshall. In connection with Marshall's remarks, he also cites the following statement from Hideyuki's book: "The middle game is an intense battle. However, this should not be without a purpose. It is often said that warm hearts and cool heads are both needed in a battlefield. Unless the strategy is always based on calm judgment of the situation, one may not be able to gain anything even if a victory is won." Hideyuki Fujisawa taught in China with a purpose. Go was born in ancient China and transmitted to Japan. China magnanimously introduced the profound game of Go to Japan. Each country has its own unique history and culture. However, histories and cultures have been interacting with one another from ancient days as they evolve and develop over time. In that sense, globalization began in ancient times. The pursuit of mutual benefits with a generous heart without falling into exclusionism is a basic principle of economics. Therein lies a sense of obligation and human empathy. Perhaps at the basis of Hideyuki's trips to China was his desire to fulfill Japan's obligation toward China. Hideyuki received Go techniques with a cool head and fulfilled Japan's ancient obligation with a warm heart. This was an international contribution by way of Go. The relationship between Japan and China has improved as a result, and the two nations gained mutual economic

---

[10] Keynes (1959: 134).

[11] Akihiko Matsui, "*fujisawa hideyuki no igo to keizai gaku atsui kokoro to reisei na zuno hampo okureno dokushojutsu*" (Game of Go and the economics of Hideyuki Fujisawa; a warm heart and a cool head: the art of reading half a step behind), *The Nihon Keizai Shimbun*, March 6, 2016, page 22.

benefits. Hideyuki had such a broad strategic vision; he was a man with a big heart. A few decades later, we still have so much to learn from Hideyuki.

Why Do Diplomats in New York Park Illegally?

In 1993, I found myself completely exhausted at the border between Côte d'Ivoire and Guinea in West Africa being stuck in a shack serving as an immigration office. I was applying to enter Guinea after traveling through a roadless tropical jungle on a shared truck. I already obtained a visa to enter Guinea while I was in Abidjan, a big city in Côte d'Ivoire. The immigration officer asked my age and nationality. When I answered, he asked my current address, place of birth, and date of birth. When I answered, he asked my parents' address, places of birth, and dates of births. When I answered, he asked various questions about my grandparents. This went on for a long time. After about an hour, I reached the limit of my physical strength. I said something that I had determined not to say: "How much do you need?" I paid the unofficial fee as instructed. I was allowed in instantly.

My experience is not all that unusual. In Africa, government officials routinely ask for bribes. Data suggest that politicians and government employees in developing countries, particularly those of Africa, are extremely corrupt. According to 2016 data from the World Bank, six of the 10 most corrupt countries are in the African continent. If culture creates values and norms, government corruption must be a reflection of culture. How does culture affect people's behavior? In a corrupt nation, people may not feel as guilty about breaking rules as people in other countries. If so, official rules are not observed in corrupt nations. However, it would be extremely difficult to validate this point. This is because people's action may be influenced by the penalties that would be imposed, rather than any feeling of guilt. The payment of penalties would be an economic cost of minor violations. Economists generally believe that people would be motivated to keep rules when they know for certain that they would be punished if they break them. Rules are different from country to country, and so are the penalties imposed for violating these rules.

American economists Raymond Fisman and Edward Miguel came up with an idea to separate two variables, the diluted guilty conscience associated with a culture of corruption, on the one hand, and the preventive potential of penal practices against rule-breaking.[12] Diplomats benefit from diplomatic immunity, which protects them from prosecutions on account of minor offenses in the country they are posted. In other words, they are not subject to the economic costs for breaking rules. New York, home of the United Nations headquarters, hosts many UN diplomats, members of various peacekeeping missions, representing countries and regions of the world. It is well known that this densely populated city is a nightmare for finding a spot to park a car. People are therefore prone to park their cars illegally. Interestingly, the New York Police Department keeps detailed records of illegal parking incidents

---

[12] Fisman and Miguel (2014).

attributed to UN diplomats. These data can reveal when, where, and by diplomats of which countries parking violations were committed. There is also a set of data that quantified the levels of national corruption across the world. Using these two sets of data, it is possible to correlate the diplomats' illegal parking behavior and the levels of corruption of their countries.

Through their statistical analysis, Fisman and Miguel obtained the following outcomes:

(1) Diplomats from high-corruption countries are more likely to park their cars illegally and not pay the parking violation penalties.
(2) Diplomats from low-corruption countries are more likely not to park their cars illegally. If they are charged for the parking violation, they tend to pay off immediately.

They claim that diplomats from countries of lower corruption levels tend to refrain from committing illegal parking. Not only that, they pay the penalties if they are ticketed, although they are in fact immune from such penalties. These diplomats bear the cost of breaking rules just like ordinary people, without exercising their rights to diplomatic immunity. This behavior defies the explanation offered by standard economics. It offers an explanation that people from the cultures that do not tolerate corruption tend to conform to rules out of their guilty conscience about violation of rules, even if they have no economic incentives. Similarly, the diplomats from the countries on friendly terms with the USA are less likely to commit parking violations, even if their countries are highly corrupt ones. It is like being on good behavior for the sake of friendship. Thus, the "*giri ninjo*," that is the sense of self-imposed indebtedness and fellow feeling, can be a key feature to soften conflicts and disputes in globalized diplomatic contexts, just as they are in the tacit rules operating in closed communities.

What Good Would It Do if Japanese Anime Was Diffused Across the World?

The theme tune of *Astro Boy* sounds on the platforms of Takadanobaba Station on a JR line in central Tokyo, signaling imminent departures of trains. Leaving the station, heading west on the Waseda dori ave., there is the former atelier of Osamu Tezuka, the author and creator of this anime hero. Here in Takadanobaba, the legendary anime creator produced many stories with iconic characters that everyone loved. As for me, I used to be a student at a university situated on the same avenue, but on the opposite side from the station. That was more than 20 years ago. In Fukuoka, there is a large panel right in front of the subway Nishijin station, across the main street from the entrance stairway. It displays an anime character, Sazae-san. The main street is named after this anime and called the Sazae-san dori avenue. Cross the road and about five minutes northward on foot, and there awaits bronze statues of Sazae-san (Fig. 2.2). These statues stand on the precincts of Seinan Gakuin University, where I

Fig. 2.2 Photograph: street sign for the Sazae-san dori avenue and bronze statues of the comic character, installed in front of the Seinan Gakuin University Library building. © Seinan Gakuin University

currently teach. The creator of this anime, Machiko Hasegawa, came up with the idea for her best-known comic while she was taking a walk along the seaside promenade not far from the university campus. Manga and anime penetrate the social fabrics of Japanese everyday life, almost regarded as legitimate members of society.

Modern Japanese culture has been globally promoted through the national branding strategy named the "Cool Japan." Manga and anime are some of the flagship cultural items. People draw on their personal experiences to form generalized ideas about other countries. If they chance upon a kind foreigner, they imagine his or her country to be full of such kind people. Impressions of a country may also be formed without meeting actual nationals of the country, but through cultural representations. Manga and anime may well be what many non-Japanese people come to know of something Japanese, and thus allow them to form their general ideas about Japan and its people. On the basis of this supposition, I decided to investigate how these Japanese cartoons and comics experienced overseas shape people's attitude toward the Japanese.[13]

I happened to be aware that, in South Korea, there was a socio-economic survey that included some questions about people's attitude toward Japanese nationals. As I was not fluent in Korean, I invited a Korean friend and long-standing fellow researcher from my graduate school days, Professor Shin Inyong of Asia University. There were three questions:

"Would you welcome Japanese people to be your neighbors?"

"Would you welcome Japanese people to be your colleagues at work?"

---

[13] Yamamura and Shin (2016).

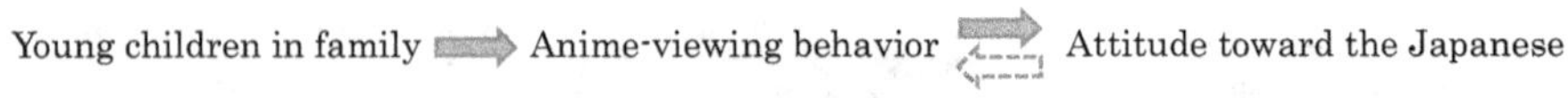

Young children in family ⟹ Anime-viewing behavior ⟸ Attitude toward the Japanese

Fig. 2.3 Mechanism of changing attitude toward the Japanese

> "Would you welcome Japanese people to be members of your family?"
>
> Each question came with two options for an answer: 1 for "yes" and 0 for "no."
>
> There was an additional question—
>
> "How often have you watched Japanese anime recently?"
>
> to which the answer could be one on a scale of 1 (none) to 4 (often). Following these questions, the survey asked whether the respondent had any children, and if they did, the ages of the children, together with some demographic data, such as household income level, respondent's gender, etc.

It is possible that those who have affinity with Japan find Japanese anime interesting, and the likelihood to watch some is therefore high. Given this possibility, it is not clear whether viewing anime at the cinema or on TV affected the viewers' attitude toward Japan. Even if a correlation can be reasonably assumed between watching Japanese cartoons and the attitudes toward the Japanese, the causal direction in this relationship cannot be ascertained—the problem that always gives economists a headache.

I already knew from another study of mine that people with young children were more likely to watch anime than those who did not.[14] To be more precise, people with the same demographic attributes, such as gender, age, and income levels, but who differ in whether they have children, exhibit a difference in how often they watch anime. This can be explained that, when the children want to watch an anime film, the adults in the family will be exposed to it, at home or the cinema, irrespective of their preferences. Anime is one of the popular conversation topics that young children like talking about with friends at nursery or school, which gives young children a strong incentive to watch it in order to be part of the conversation, and therefore the shared comradery. For the parents, they would not want their child to be left out, and they end up watching the anime with the child after all. If this hypothesis of anime-viewing behavior applies to Korean society, then the following relationships can be assumed. This is illustrated in Fig. 2.3:

Statistically, the influence of anime-viewing to the attitude toward the Japanese can be verified given that young children in a family prompt anime-viewing, but they themselves do not determine the attitude toward Japanese people. An analysis based on this framework yielded the following outcomes:

(1) Parents with children aged under 12 are more likely to view anime films/programs, and
(2) The frequency of anime-viewing corresponds to the level of acceptance toward the Japanese as neighbors or colleagues, but is irrelevant to their acceptance in terms of family inclusion.

---

[14] Yamamura (2014).

It seems to follow that watching anime stimulates preferable ideas about the Japanese in the Korean psyche, helping to develop a more accepting mood in Korean society. However, family inclusion is a matter that directly concerns the issue of self-identity and thus people's opinions do not seem to be swayed so easily by simply viewing some anime.

I wonder if manga and anime will be integrated into the fabric of everyday life outside Japan, as it has been in the lives of Japanese people. The international politics in 2019, shaken by the Trump administration, shifted from collaboration to conflict. The international diplomacy between Japan and South Korea has also turned antagonistic. A moral judgment requires careful considerations. Some may think the "right" judgment has to be made at all human and material cost. But the "right" decision may differ from country to country, not necessarily representing a universal "righteousness." This makes me recall a very famous line from the manga *Golgo 13* by Takao Saito, "That justice is your justice and yours only, isn't it?" It epitomizes this so eloquently. In order to avoid a clash of different "justices," let us share a joy of something simple in our familiar domain and devoid of politics. Cool Japan has the potential to transcend the culturally specific "moral judgment." To my mind, it can diffuse in people's minds over a long period of time. In this sense, culture offers a ray of hope in this modern world that increasingly veers toward exclusivism.

What Was It in "Oshin" that Won the Hearts and Minds of People Overseas?

As I mentioned earlier, I was traveling the world as a budget backpacker in my twenties. In countries where Japanese travelers were few, people would come and speak to me out of curiosity. One day in Egypt, in 1993, I was on a bus in Cairo. A man in Egyptian traditional attire with a handsome beard approached me and called out to me, "Oswin." I had no idea what he wanted to say. Soon, other Egyptians on the bus gathered joining him, repeating the same word as they spoke. I finally figured out that they were calling a name "Oshin," a fictitious female character featured in a drama series with a namesake title, aired on NHK originally in 1983 to 1984. I asked them to confirm my hunch, which delighted them. These people, young and old alike, say "we are so proud of Oshin," one after another, with big smiles smeared all over their faces. I joined the bandwagon and said, "Japan is proud of Oshin." It was a happy bus ride. I remember, when I finally reached my destination, I shook hands with everyone, saying good-byes.

A few months later, I was in the Paraguayan capital of Asunción, literally on the other side of the planet from Japan. As I waited for my coach at a terminal for long-distance services, I noticed a TV playing in the terminal building. I recognized something familiar was on the screen. It was a girl clothed in the Japanese style. The backdrop was an all-white snowscape, and she was drifting on a flimsy raft, down the river away from the screen. She cries out, tears streaming down on her cheeks. A woman, seemingly the girl's mother, was watching from the riverbank, also crying. I recognized this tear-jerking scene of parting. This was an iconic scene from the NHK drama, *Oshin*, as I watched it in my early teenage years. I remember vaguely that the title spelled as "Ocin" in rainbow colors adorning the top right corner of the coach station TV monitor. On occasions during my trip, I saw the program being broadcast in other regions. I was deeply impressed by witnessing that this tear-jerking story of hardship and humanity represented through the portrayal of resilient people of northeast Japan, this somber story set in rural, early-twentieth-century Japan, touched the heartstrings of people both in Islamic and Christian societies.

The lead character Oshin is a Japanese woman, born in Yamagata in 1901, into a poor peasant family. She was a young studious girl, but poverty forced the family to send her away as a child laborer. Her life then was a chain of hardships. She was not allowed to attend school. She was accused of wrongdoing by her employer, which she did not commit. One snowy day, she decided to flee. Being a homeless refugee, she nearly died of cold, but she was rescued by a man, who later taught her how to read and write. Many other challenges awaited her in her life, but she survived with her resilience and determination. Eventually, she became a successful business owner in her adulthood.

Nobel laureate professor James Heckman points out the importance of education in early childhood.[15] He conducted a project to investigate the effects of early education initiative called the Perry Preschool Project in impoverished American communities. This is a 40-year longitudinal study of children who had received education and those who had not. It revealed that the children with education demonstrated higher educational attainment (cognitive abilities). In addition, these children showed higher levels of perseverance (non-cognitive skills). These effects were long-lasting well into the children's adulthood and led to a lower chance of criminal behavior. This study was characterized by its focus on the importance of education in early childhood development and the emphasis on non-cognitive skills. Coming back to our Oshin, she did not receive formal education, but she underwent a kind of education in her childhood, and perhaps, all the hardship in her life gave her the chance to develop necessary non-cognitive skills.

The early twentieth century, when Oshin spent her childhood, was a completely different epoch from the viewpoint of our modern Japanese society, in which most ordinary children find themselves today. The proverb "if you love your child, send him away," which would be roughly an equivalent of the English proverb "spare the rod and spoil the child," might have made good sense in olden days, but today this is an impossibility. Who would be willing to risk their child falling in the hands of a kidnapper? Today, children must be provided with safe environments. The effectiveness of group learning at school has been well-proven.[16] However, non-cognitive skills involve social skills and collaborative disposition, which the closed community within a school may not be able to fully nurture. These skills may possibly be developed through personal experiences outside school. This is precisely the point we take

---

[15] Heckman (2015).

[16] These include Algan et al. (2013) and Ito et al. (2021).

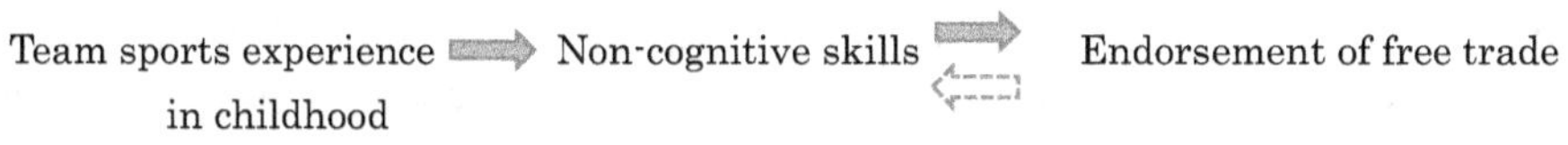

Team sports experience in childhood ⟹ Non-cognitive skills ⇄ Endorsement of free trade

Fig. 2.4 Effect of team sports experience

away from the "Oshin" story. And this led me to the question, how can non-cognitive skills be developed? To find out, I conducted a study, jointly with Professor Emeritus Yoshiro Tsutsui of Osaka University.[17] Our hypothesis can be expressed in the chart below (Fig. 2.4).

Children would understand the value of collaboration and cooperation with others and experience it through being a member of a team in sport. They would also learn from the experience of competition. Through competition, they would find out what they were good at or what they should pursue in their lives.[18] For example, a child may lack talent in music and yet aim to be a pianist. If this child had no competitors around him, he may carry on trying to be a pianist until it is too late to change the course of his life to be something else. Conversely, if he is placed in a competitive environment, he would come to recognize his relative lack of competence and start looking for a more appropriate pursuit for him. Team sports also give children opportunities to expand the horizon of their socialization beyond the limited circle of their schools as they compete with teams from other schools. Individual sports are good for learning the meaning of competition in itself and the value of efforts for self-improvement, but from the viewpoint of social skills, team sports would better serve for this purpose. These "skills for life" attained in the social context will eventually help the children recognize such things as the benefits derived from mutual relationships in open and free trade and the profits generated through international competition.

We conducted a study to investigate the extent to which our hypothesis mentioned above explained the reality. Approximately 10,000 people participated in a survey, which involved questions about the following: (1) experience of individual sports and team sports in elementary school; (2) their non-cognitive skills in terms of collaborative disposition, reciprocity, trusting disposition, and understanding of the significance of competition[19]; and (3) opinions about free trade.[20] The results are summarized as follows:

---

[17] Yamamura and Tsutsui (2019a).

[18] A study found that people who had anti-competitive education at elementary school were likely to show poorer performance in terms of "trust in others," "collaboration," and "reciprocity" (Ito et al. 2021).

[19] Participants were asked to give their responses to statements by giving a score between 1 (strongly disagree) and 5 (strongly agree). The statements were as follows: (1) Group tasks bring about positive results; (2) A person did me a favor, and I should reciprocate the favor; (3) I find most people trustworthy; and (4) Competition is beneficial to society.

[20] The question asked participants to give a score about a statement about free trade between 5 (strongly agree) and 1 (strongly disagree).

(1) Experience in team sports has positive impacts on all of the collaborative disposition, reciprocity, trusting disposition, and understanding of the significance of competition,
(2) Experience in individual sports only has positive impacts on the understanding of the significance of competition, and
(3) All of the collaborative disposition, reciprocity, trusting disposition, and understanding of the significance of competition were positive factors for prompting agreement with the statement about free trade.

These results suggest that children broaden their perspectives and foster perseverance through playing sports in teams. Winning is not everything in playing sports. A player must first compete with their peers to be selected as a team member for a game. In the tournament, they eventually experience defeat. There is always a champion, but it would be impossible to be a winner in every tournament they play. It can be assumed that people who have played in team sports have an experience of losing a game. It means that they have learned what it means to be a loser. They may develop more strategies to win as a team. They will then play against teams from other schools, against strangers. All these experiences will foster social skills in the children and teach them the meaning of winning as well as losing. They develop resilience—if they lose, they try harder so that they will win next time.

We find many "Oshins" in contemporary Japan. A prominent one is perhaps Nobel laureate Dr. Shinya Yamanaka. As a young man, he was into rugby. Injuries were not infrequent. When he started an internship program to become a surgeon, his clumsiness garnered him a nickname "Dumb-naka." Later, he changed his career path to research. He also studied abroad. When he returned to Japan, he grew laboratory animals himself in order to economize his research funding and eventually suffered depression. After the Nobel prize, he experienced bereavement, and his research was thrown into a scandal.[21] Despite all these adversities, Dr. Yamanaka always maintains composure and keeps moving forward. His eventful life and undeterred perseverance remind me of Oshin.

In May 2019, Japan celebrated the beginning of a new imperial era named "Reiwa." The first My Personal History section on the Nihon Keizai Shimbun featured Sugako Hashida, the script writer who created *Oshin*. Hashida reveals that the name Oshin resonates with the truth, wholeheartedness, and principle, all of which have "shin" in their respective Japanese words. It is, according to her, a name that represents a woman who makes her way steadfastly through a winding path of life.[22] The script writer recalls that, when the famous scene of the parting of mother and daughter was successfully shot, "everyone, the crew and galleries together, roared with applause, their faces wet with tears. Among them, I was also sobbing." The broadcast that year, 1983, was a huge success with the top viewing rate marking

---

[21] Yamanaka et al. (2017).
"Nobel-winner Professor Yamanaka rises above the iPS research paper forgery devastation" on AERA dot. Website, published on January 31, 2018 (in Japanese). https://dot.asahi.com/aera/2018013000027.html (accessed January 15, 2019).

[22] 'My Personal History Ver. 21', *The Nihon Keizai Shimbun*, May 22, 2019.

62.9%. Subsequently, the drama was broadcast in 68 countries and regions worldwide.[23] Moreover, the viewing rates were "as high as 82% in Iran, 81% in Thailand, and 76% in Beijing. The woman who endures, who never gives up her hopes, who maintains her humanity intact no matter the situation, reached people's hearts and minds despite the differences in languages, religious affiliations…"[24] The Oshin story, a tale of a woman who lived a full life through the tumultuous times of twentieth century Japan, even touches the heartstrings of younger generations of today.[25] It has the power to inspire people of all kinds, genders, nationalities, and religious beliefs, and it also has timeless authenticity. Oshin continues to live in the twenty-first century in the minds of more and more people around the world.

Do Children's Values Reflect Their Parents' Values?

The ever globalizing world of the twenty-first century faces divided public opinions about the issue of immigrants. In Europe, Brexit is stirring turmoil and giving rise to nationalism and exclusivism. The USA, the epicenter of economics, is populated mostly by immigrants and their descendants, and its most prominent city is *New* York. The incumbent president Donald Trump, while pursuing exclusivist economic policies, himself comes from a family of German immigrants. The issue of immigrants thus is a hot topic for economic analysis to consider the future of the world.

Among many existing economic empirical studies, one conducted by Yann Algan and Pierre Cahuc is worth casting our eyes to.[26] The US population is largely accounted for by immigrant-descendants though indigenous people do exist. They are all American nationals today, but their roots are diverse. Algan and Cahuc investigated the typical values and views of the immigrants' ancestral countries of origin and analyzed their impact on those of Americans today. They found that people whose ancestors came from a country which had high tendencies to trust others also exhibited more trusting disposition, and that higher levels of trust corresponded with higher economic wealth levels. Even under equal current conditions, the values inherited from previous generations have bearing on the outcomes of the lives of descendants. A pioneering study in social psychology goes even further to analyze the conditions under which the ancestral values were formed.[27] In southern parts of the USA, there is the so-called culture of honor, which regards violence as a legitimate means to

---

[23] 'My Personal History Ver. 22', *The Nihon Keizai Shimbun*, May 23, 2019.

[24] 'My Personal History Ver. 23', *The Nihon Keizai Shimbun*, May 24, 2019.

[25] *Oshin* was rerun in its entirety on the NHK satellite channel in 2019 as Japan moved from the "Heisei" era to the new "Reiwa" era. A newspaper reported, "Many viewers must be shedding sympathetic tears every morning as they watch its episodes. … At present, the story is coming to the climax of Oshin's youth, played by the actress Ayako Kobayashi. … Tweets by seemingly the Generation Z pop up incessantly: 'the episode was heartbreaking,' 'they've done it again,' 'made me cry,' etc." ('Shunju', *The Nihon Keizai Shimbun* April 1, 2019: 1).

[26] Algan and Cahuc (2010).

[27] Nisbett and Cohen (2009).

counter insults. In this culture, it is normal, and even important, to constantly send out the message that you are "not to be messed with." It draws a stark contrast with the culture of northern parts of America, inhabited by many social elites living in cities such as Boston. This culture of honor is attributed to the locals' ancestral roots, that many came from pastoral farming families of Ulster Scots from the British Isles. There, their relatively small communities lacked official law-enforcement authorities. People were poor, and food scarce, unlike crop-growers. The temptation to steal livestock was palpable. It was therefore a first rule of survival that one must keep up a guard at all times. The norms for Ulster Scots were thus formed out of the geopolitical necessity. The social norms were perpetuated by those Scotch-Irish people over generations in their migrated land of America. In their communities, you will be seen as "chickened out" if you do not launch an immediate counterattack upon someone who insults you. Failing this, people will disrespect you, and your social standing will suffer. One needs to have a reactional impulse to strike "like a man" to maintain one's dignity. A display of fearless payback will earn you the admiration, respect, and trust from others. The culture of honor is kept alive and shared in this way among men and women, young and old. Such a culture paints the backdrop of pro-gun-society advocates, who assert that people need to protect themselves.

It is not only the south where the culture of honor, or something similar, prevails in the United States. It thrives in the areas where the decline of automobile and other industries left even white Americans in poverty, known as the "Rust Belt," and the predominant ideology embraces violence, like the culture of honor of the south. The memoir written by James D. Vance became a bestseller in the United States after Donald Trump won the presidential election.[28] The early life, upbringing, and values of this Ohio-born author provide a rich source of information to understand the psychology behind the people who support the Trump administration. It illustrates an aspect of this country that is hardly reported by the Japanese media. President Trump understood and appealed to the sentiments of the "forgotten white people." Nevertheless, the situations for these people are unlikely to change no matter what "radical" policies the president concocts. There is no chance that the violence-central values find a place in American leadership or global society. Are they, then, destined to be disrespected and scoffed at by the social elites and left behind by the social majority? Vance's life story offers a hopeful clue. He graduated from Yale Law School, qualified as a solicitor, and today he manages an investment firm in Silicon Valley. He is one of America's young business elites, well connected to the country's ruling class. His grandmother, a rather wild woman, regarded education very important, and she made sure that young James understood it and supported him. Before Yale Law School, Vance lived in a world nothing to do with elites, but he secured a scholarship grant to be admitted at this prestigious institution, and he studied hard. Eventually, his grandmother's principle on education bore fruit in what he has become. As it was discussed earlier in this section, childhood education and development helped to change the course of his life, and today he is a person who can make rational responses without resorting to violence in a situation where his dignity is at stake.

---

[28] Vance (2017).

He is now married to a gentle and intelligent woman. James Vance will start a new family history.

At university, I learned about the notion of habitus put forth by French sociologist Pierre Bourdieu.[29] To put it simply, this is an idea that people's preferences and habits in life are significantly influenced by shared values in their families and communities. These shared values are the habitus. People think, behave, and make decisions according to their habitus. Communities of such people are distinct and never merge with one another. Their inhabitants live in an exclusive world without crossing the borders. This is the gist of the notion, if, admittedly, it is a wild simplification. Bourdieu came from a provincial town in France. His grandparents were farmers, and his father only had primary education. It was at an elite school in Paris that he first experienced a completely different circle of people and their society. With his provincial accent, he felt belittled in front of "sophisticated" Parisians, and he also felt uneasy with the "elite" anthropologists of this capital city and their arrogance with which they studied rural communities such as his own. These experiences, apparently, inspired him to formulate the notion of habitus.

As an economist, I recognize the value of the market system and competition, and to my mind, creating a more functional system seems almost impossible. However, I feel weary toward the "economists" who advance this idea with their typical "superiority." It is one thing that economists discuss economic systems among themselves, propounding clear and precise definitions. However, they could not get their ideas across to ordinary people if they did not change the language they use. Otherwise, people would feel troubled not by what they said, but by how they said it. This is by virtue of people's humanity aspect that is responding to the manner which reveals the intension behind those words rather than to the content. In the 2016 US presidential election, the media initially paid but a scanty attention to Donald Trump as a material competitor. But what they overlooked was the existence of the "forgotten white people" of America. They were made aware of the power of sympathy and influence of these people through Mr. Trump's victory, as he managed to win over the support from this segment of the American population, which both the liberal and conservative camps took no notice of. It turned out that he knew better than anyone the potential power of the perpetual culture of honor. This should be an epiphany for scholarly economists.

I must confess that I myself put on the "superiority" robe when I speak about economic policies and such to the general public. I become aware of it at another level of consciousness, then I throw bits and bobs in my talk to dilute the arrogance. This is the secret ingredient to make academic work rich and tasteful so that it speaks to people also on the level of their humanity.

---

[29] Bourdieu (1991).

What Changes if Fukuzawa Yukichi is Shown on a 10,000-Yen Bill?

Shotoku Taishi, a man whose portrait is printed on a banknote of 10,000 yen—who is this man? As exhibited in Fig. 2.5, a mysterious figure who holds a wooden bar in his hands, wearing an oversized shirt and a strange hat. It makes no sense. The banknote makes no sense, for I have nothing to do with this amount of money. I am more familiar with Mr. Iwakura Tomomi, who adorns 500-yen bills, my pocket money. As exhibited in Fig. 2.6, his hair neatly combed back, he is a nice-looking gentleman in a suit and bow-tie. This is what I used to think as a schoolboy.

Fig. 2.5 An old 10,000 yen bill with a portrait of Shotoku Taishi, the bill is no longer in circulation (Left). A portrait of Shotoku Taishi (Right). © PIXTA

Fig. 2.6 A 500 yen bill with a portrait of Iwakura Tomomi, the bill is no longer in circulation (Left). A portrait of Iwakura (Right). © PIXTA

Time elapsed, and the 500 yen bills have been replaced by coins. The 10,000 yen note has also been remodeled with Fukuzawa Yukichi. This is a distinguished-looking man in Kimono, with his hair pushed backward. Unlike Shotoku Taishi, he has a dignified air about him. A 1,000 yen bill features Hideyo Noguchi, who is portrayed with long curly hair side-parted, and a mustache, attired in a jacket and tie. I wonder if his hair was naturally curly, or he had it styled at a hair salon. In any case, he has a look that one might find among one's university professors.

The portraits most familiar to the modern Japanese people are the ones on banknotes. These are eminent figures in Japanese history. I have the feeling that persona on higher denomination notes has a more otherworldly aura. The 10,000 yen bill with Shotoku Taishi was introduced in November 1958, and on November 1, 1984, Mr. Fukuzawa replaced him. The banknotes were further renewed on November 1, 2004, with new figures representing different denomination bills. The 5,000 yen bill has Ichiyo Higuchi, a female literary author of the late-nineteenth century. Having her on a banknote was symbolic of the changing social status of women in Japan. She is depicted in kimono, and her hair is tied in the traditional *mage* style. She has a beautiful, sophisticated countenance. Fukuzawa Yukichi, for some reason, survived this latest design revamp and 10,000 yen notes with his face on them are in circulation today. On extant photographs of him, Fukuzawa portrays various persona—sometimes a man in the samurai attire with a top-knot, a sword on his waist, or a modernized man in Western clothing and combed, parted hair. My grandfather, born in 1866, moved from a rural town in Kochi to Tokyo in 1886 to study at the Keio Gijuku (present-day Keio University). At that time, Fukuzawa was 50 years old, and perhaps looked just like the portrait on the banknote. My great-grandfather must have met or seen him in person. He could have been in casual company of this professor. I wonder how he would come across to my grandfather. Would he be attired in modern suit and tie, or in kimono? I wish I had a time machine to verify this private thought of mine…

His contemporary era saw a great deal of changes in society, fashion, and lifestyle, inspired by the culture brought in from the West. The influence must also have extended to people's thoughts. Fukuzawa Yukichi was an influential figure, an advocate of *"De-Asianization"* and the author of *An Encouragement of Learning*, who inspired social reform in Japan. Many aspiring young people left their hometowns, hoping to be his students in Tokyo. Then, I have a question from my viewpoint as an economist of the modern era.

Did scholarly education based on academic disciplines of the West change the values of the Japanese?

There is no doubt that formal education had a significant influence on Fukuzawa Yukichi, who himself became an educator. However, in the early twentieth century, only a few affluent people could have access to higher education. Japanese society is not by and large dictated by a few elites, like the high society of France. In Japan, it appears to me, the fundamental drive comes from the majority of commoners. I wonder if, by any chance, the value system prevalent among the Japanese underwent a change before the education became widely available to ordinary people. Imagine, changes in lifestyles might lead to physical changes, like people who would sit directly on the floor with bent knees start sitting on chairs, and their physique might gradually develop like that of white Caucasians, taller with longer legs. When the eye levels are elevated, it might change their perspectives and, hence, ideas. This thought leads to another question: "Can changes in the physical environment result in changes in people's values?".

A group of economist researchers conducted a study recently to address this question, using a large volume of data.[30] They firstly calculated how much of a country's economic activities are accounted for by trade with one particular country. For example, how much the Japan-US trade accounts for against Japan's GDP. Then, cultural perceptions are compared between those of the Japanese and the Americans. For this, they drew on the World Value Surveys to quantify the typical values held by different countries.[31] With these data, the difference in cultural values between Japan and USA is calculated. The same calculation is repeated to create a set of data for Japan with many other countries. In the study, they extracted data from 31 countries and prepared sets of data on the dissimilarities of personal values in relation to bilateral trade. This means there were 30 pairs for Japan alone. With the data for all countries prepared, the authors of the study analyzed the relationship between the proportion of one particular bilateral trade against the country's entire economy and the differences in cultural values between the two countries. This is then interpreted as the degree to which predominant values in one country are influenced by the goods that come from another specific country. And this is what the study found:

(1) The share of bilateral trade in one country's total economic activities corresponds to the degree to which the two countries differ from one another in terms of people's personal values.

This suggests that engaging in international trade with another country has an implication to the personal values of people that they assimilate to those of the other country. The study further classified the trade into two types: for items that are more or less universal (homogeneous goods) and ones that come with unique attributes in different countries (heterogeneous goods). For example, apparel items differ from country to country in terms of popular designs, mainstream fabrics, and so on. Thus, these are classified as heterogeneous goods. On the basis of this dichotomous classification of merchandise, they found that:

(2) The share of bilateral trade in homogeneous goods in one country's total economic activities has no implications on the degree of dissimilarity of values between the two countries, and

---

[30] Maystre et al. (2014).

[31] The surveys measure values of a particular nation by synthesizing responses to 30 questions which represent various variables: the questions refer to the extent to which respondents trust others, how often they discuss politics with friends, how much they respect their parents, how much they feel responsible for their children, and to what extent they believe freedom of speech should be protected, among other topics.

(3) The share of bilateral trade in heterogeneous goods in one country's total economic activities corresponds to the degree of similarity in people's values between the two countries.

People's values undergo a gradual change to somewhat assimilate to those of foreign countries through the exposure to the exotic goods imported from these countries—the goods that are new to them. From the viewpoint of standard economics, international trade levels out prices of goods across the world. What the study findings tell us is that imported goods open up new perspectives to people, enabling them to begin to understand the ideas behind these items, i.e., the ways in which people of the goods' original countries think.

To apply these findings to the context in which Japan was undergoing the social and political renaissance in the early twentieth century, we can imagine that Fukuzawa experienced a transformation of his values as he switched his top-knot and sword to combed hair and a tailored suit. He then became an advocate of de-Asianization. Today, he gazes at every individual who takes a 10,000 yen note in their hands. A study of behavioral economics suggests that people change their behavior without the awareness of it when they are exposed to an image—a painting, poster, etc.—that depicts human eyes.[32] Being gazed at from the banknote, we may be unknowingly absorbing Fukuzawa's worldviews. Even dead, Fukuzawa Yukichi continues to address Japanese people about broadening their horizon, that is, into the new era of globalization.

---

[32] According to Bateson et al. (2012), incidents of bicycle theft fell more than 50% when posters depicting "watching eyes" were displayed above bicycle racks.

Chapter 3
Why Is It a Secret to Successful Business Management That the Business Owner Treats Job-Seekers to Gourmet Food?

As a resident of Fukuoka, I find myself excited being in Tokyo on occasional business trips. The first thing I do on arrival is to find a noodle stand. Noodle stands are small establishments with a long high counter, at which customers consume their orders standing. They are frequented by office workers, freelancers, and other people from different walks of life, and they are all focused on their bowls of noodles, making slurping noises, but not a single word. I join them quietly and tuck in, squeezing my shoulders so as not to knock my neighbors with my elbows. This *is* Tokyo. On one occasion, I found Fujisoba, a famous stand-style noodle restaurant chain, near Ochanomizu Station. As I entered, I noticed a poster on the wall, advertising a book entitled "Why does Fujisoba pay bonuses to part-timers?"[1] I gathered that it was written by the enterprise's president. The catch copy read, "Why is it that *enka* is always playing in the background in Fujisoba restaurants?" As I was reading these words, I suddenly realized that, in fact, this shop was playing *enka*, melancholic ballade-style Japanese songs. With my curiosity aroused, I found a bookstore nearby and bought a copy of this Fujisoba book.

Mr. Tan, the president of this restaurant chain, claims that "a little overpayment of wage goes a long way." Conventionally, increased wages push up labor cost and put a strain on the business finance. If it escalates, business survival may be at stake. According to a standard theory of economics, therefore, employers do not pay employees more than the amount they deserve for their contributions. This theory must presuppose that employee performance is closely monitored and verified. However, this is not practical, as it is impossible for managers to keep an eye on their workers all the time or ensure that sales representatives are not killing time in cafes instead of visiting clients. Another tenet of the standard theory presupposes that wages are invariable across companies. Lazy employees may be fired, but they can find the same jobs in another company. In other words, there is always a chance that some of new recruits are time-wasters. In this way, a company can never get rid of procrastinating employees completely. The real world, in a nutshell, is not so

---

[1] Tan (2017: Chap. 2).

simple as the standard theory illustrates. This has given rise to a new, efficiency wage hypothesis. It acknowledges the rationale of rewarding employees with more than their fair contributions.[2] The reason being that they would lose out by being sacked for procrastination when jobs at other companies do not pay as much. Therefore, the remuneration policy of Fujisoba makes sense.

The Fujisoba president's narrative includes many episodes from his life experience that cannot be understood solely by "rational" explanations. For example, he used to run an estate agency and was paying his employees twice as much as the average wage in the industry. When job-seekers came to the company for an interview, Mr. Tan would take them to a restaurant for a hearty treat, such as crunchy deep-fried pork cutlets and teriyaki-grilled eels. These are mere candidates. There is no guarantee that they will come and work for him. But surprisingly, the president treated everyone equally, without favoring one over another, including those who did not appear as promising talents. Meanwhile, it is possible that buying candidate employees a dinner may be considered as a means to promote an enhanced corporate image. In this sense, the efficiency wage hypothesis stands as it would make sense to choose a "lucrative" job and stay in employment. However, there is another crucial element in what he did. Mr. Tan the president of a company must be a busy man, but he took time out to eat with people who were practically strangers. He must have had some other, more important or profitable businesses to attend to, but he sacrificed such profits for the opportunity to eat with the job seekers. His behavior, then, can be understood to reflect his anticipatory belief in the potential of people who wish to work for his company. It is in a way a palpable expression of his expectation that these possibly prospective employees will produce more value and profit than the engagements at hand that have been subordinated. Mr. Tan had in his mind the idea that, one day, the repayment for the indebtedness would be greater than what they received. Drawing on his experience, he analyzes that "there have been more than a few employees who flourished despite having come across not particularly competent at first, which may as well be explained by the treated dinner that was catalytic." In economics terms, the pre-employment complimentary dinner causes sentimental debt owed to the company president, which stimulates the employee's motivation, leading to their enhanced performance. As a result, the company realizes better business performance.

There are studies into the mechanisms of sentimental indebtedness and attachment being pursued in disciplines such as social psychology and economics. Let me introduce an economic experiment called the ultimatum game. In this game, two individuals, call them A and B, have a prospect of sharing 10,000 yen between them. Participant A has the right to decide the distribution of shares and make a proposition to B. Upon hearing A's proposition, B has the right to decide whether it is acceptable. The rule is that the proposed shares will be handed to them if B accepts the proposition, but they get nothing if B rejects it. Standard economics presupposes that individuals are focused on their own gains, disregarding the interest of others. It follows that any amount is a gain, so that B would accept A's proposition unless

---

[2] The explanation of the efficiency wage hypothesis is based on Sasaki (2011).

it is 100:0. If this is the case, and if A knows it, then A would propose 9,999:1 to maximize his own profit. He may want to take all of it, but B would dismiss such a proposition, in which case A would lose the whole amount. Therefore, A would not consider this option. This game has been tested in many countries across the world. In many cases, A suggests a little more than a half for his share, and B accepts this. The greater the proportion of A's share becomes, the more likely that B rejects the proposition, knowing that the latter will also gain nothing. This behavior clearly defies the hypothetical persona postulated by standard economics. People opt to sacrifice their own interests in order to maintain an equal standing rather than to concede to gross inequality that disadvantages them. When this behavior is diffused in society, there emerges a consensus that extreme inequality must be avoided.

These results of the economics tests seem to explain the fundamental reason for Carlos Ghosn's downfall. He, and corporate executives in general, may also learn from the history of democracy. According to the economist Peter Leeson, the world's first democracy came into being on a pirate ship.[3] There, a captain is chosen democratically by selecting one who is the most competent in leadership to maximize the profit efficiently. This is analogous to appointing the most competent business manager to a CEO in the corporate context. Interestingly on the pirate ship, the profit is distributed equally. The captain takes an equal amount to those of others. If the captain gains more than crew members, they will harbor discontent, which may lead to an elimination of the captain. While corporate CEOs may be condemned or prosecuted, their lives are at least safe. In the world of pirates, however, it is a life-or-death situation where raw desires and violence are uncontrolled. Therefore, egoistic behaviors are inhibited. Business owners should be aware of this aspect of the fundamental humanity of individuals.

Now, here is a dilemma. If high-performing employees are not paid proportionately for their performance, their morale may suffer, and so will the business performance of the company. This is at least true in the standard economics paradigm. However, a company is an organization, which requires team efforts. No star employee can boost the company performance without the support of his or her colleagues. Then, which hypothesis is correct? To gain an insight into this question, I looked at the Japan Professional Football League and analyzed how the disparities in annual salaries among team members affected the overall team performance. The results revealed that, at least before the country's football competence was pushed up to the world's standard levels, larger disparities in a team corresponded with poorer winning rates.[4] Back to Mr. Tan of Fujisoba, he learned this from his mother, who said to him, "If you want to run a business, you need to know the secret of success: one, **never monopolize the profit,** and two, **distribute it equally to everyone**. Otherwise, you will have no gain in the end."[5] These maxims keep Fujisoba restaurants in business.

---

[3] Leeson (2011).
[4] Yamamura (2015).
[5] Tan (2017: Chap. 1).

The readers may wonder, "supposing that the company Fujisoba operates under a socialist ideology, how can it exercise innovative creativity?" Well, Fujisoba does not show any signs of stagnation like socialist states did in the past. As it will be described in *How does ninjo (human sentiments) enrich the market economy?* below, the socialist regimes were administered by privileged classes, contrary to their egalitarian claim. Moreover, a social control through mutual surveillance restrained people's freedom. Whereas, the Fujisoba company does not provide a separate president office as in a room. Mr. Tan does not allow special treatments for him, so when he pays a visit to one of their restaurants to eat as well as to inspect, he must be treated as one of the customers. He believes that self-importance and narcissistic entitlement cause nothing but harm to the business. Fujisoba is a liberal company. Its employees can turn up to work in jeans and polo shirts. They are allowed to leave office for personal errands during the office hours as long as the work is properly managed, for example, by notifying the boss and ensuring someone to stand in. The company's product development is an all-participatory affair, welcoming ideas from everyone, and interesting ideas are appreciated even if they are not approved for production. Even the most far-fetched ideas will not be met with negative feedback. This environment has enabled the development of blockbuster products, such as their unique "Tornado Potato Soba noodle." Original ideas for successful products could come from anyone, so the basic idea is to broaden the scope of catchment. Without a doubt, this naturally boosts employees' morale. With freedom and equality combined in equilibrium, the result is a corporate culture that drives innovation. President Tan's management philosophy offers a research topic for studies of the most advanced economics—**business managers' responsibility is to think about how to motivate employees and create an employee-centric workplace**.

Social psychologist Tatsuya Kameda of the University of Tokyo submits a possibility that "a softie is the ultimate winner."[6] A company like Fujisoba effortlessly garners positive customer reviews, which in turn help to establish and promote the corporate brand in the market. This leads to enhanced business performance, and thus generates a profitable cycle. A business owner may strategically pretend to be a "nice guy" in anticipation of gaining access to this cycle, but such a cunning man is always at the risk of unwittingly making a revealing mistake. A man of sentimentality, by contrast, is immune from this risk because there is no scheming in the first place. A person may suffer small, temporary setbacks from his generous acts by indulging in his/her self-imposed sense of duty and sentimental compassion, but ultimately, he/she has a great chance of being admired by community members and, in the context of a competitive market, succeed to survive. An illustrative portrayal of this persona can be found in Tora-san, a happy-go-lucky character played by actor Kiyoshi Atsumi in a long-run movie series, *Otoko wa tsurai yo* (it's tough being a man) from the good old Showa times. His genuine, uncalculating personality must be the reason the series captured the hearts and minds of people, enabling the long, successful enterprise despite the declining popularity of the cinema industry.

---

[6] Information concerning this paragraph was taken from Kameda (2017: Chap. 3).

The reason for Fujisoba restaurants to play enka, Mr. Tan explains, is to sympathize, through its blues-esque lyrics, with customers, who may be going through a hardship, hoping that the songs will offer consolation, courage, and strength to confront whatever the situation may be. In other words, the choice of enka is a compassionate message of encouragement and support.

How Is the French Mentality Relevant to the Arrest of Carlos Ghosn?

In November 2018, the then-chairman of Nissan Motor Co., Mitsubishi Motors, and Renault SA, Carlos Ghosn was arrested. He was suspected to have underreported his compensation of approximately 2 billion yen by about a half of the amount, just 1 billion. Some speculate that the man, internationally acclaimed as a powerful business leader, underreported his compensation in order to avoid social criticisms about his astounding income. But, given that Nissan is a private corporation, his primary objective should be to make the company grow its profit, and if Ghosn made significant contributions toward this cause and his compensation was proportionate, there should be no problems. What he could have done is to declare his income truthfully and justify himself to the company shareholders. He has been reported to claim that he deserved the high compensation, only after he was arrested.

If so, what was the reason that prompted him to misrepresent his income? Take a look at a study which compared several nations on the topic of an ideal society. In the study, two ideas are proposed: a middle-class society in which wealth is relatively evenly distributed and an elitist society which involves significant economic inequalities. Table 3.1 shows the percentages of people who consider either type of

Table 3.1 Ideal and actual states of society (%)

Middle-class society	Ideal	Actual	Gap
Japan	56	20	−36
France	50	12	−38
Denmark	60	59	−1
Sweden	52	38	−14
Elitist society	Ideal	Actual	Gap
Japan	9	39	30
France	6	54	48
Denmark	2	11	9
Sweden	3	23	20

Note The middle-class society is defined as "a society whose majority comprises medium income earners" while the elitist society as "a society that is inhabited by a small number of high-earning elites and the majority of low-income population"

society as ideal, and also who consider that one of the ideas describe their society in reality. The difference between the two figures indicates the perceived gap between the ideal and the reality. As points of reference, data about Denmark and Sweden, known as welfare states, are included. More than half of people in every country responded positively to the middle-class society as an ideal. Whereas, interestingly, their opinions about the middle-class society representing the reality are divided. In Japan and France, not many people thought their societies were egalitarian, prevailed by middle-class population, suggesting greater gaps between the ideal and the reality than those perceived by northern European people. Meanwhile, the elitist society is not popular in all these countries. It is noteworthy that, in France, the majority considered their society to be an elitist one. The gap is far greater than that among the Japanese. As for Denmark and Sweden, the levels of discrepancy are low. Overall, France stands out by far for their perceptual gap between the ideal and real societies. Japan shows a similar result to France, for few responded to the idea that they live in a middle-class society in reality. However, the negative reaction to the idea of social elites is not as strong as in France.[7] I imagine that the national resentment against elites is closely related to people's values deeply rooted in the post-revolution national motto of "liberty, equality, and fraternity."

It is likely that Mr. Ghosn's income is far higher than most people, who would then feel resentful toward him no matter how significant the businessman's contributions might be, given the staggering disparity. It is not difficult to imagine that the disclosure of his true income level would be met with disdain from the French public. This is indicated in economics studies as well: people's levels of satisfaction in life decline inversely proportionately to the income levels of other people around them.[8] There is a growing number of people who argue that disparity in income levels is growing rapidly. There is a remarkable accumulation of data on the subject contributed by French economists, perhaps reflecting the characteristic national mentality. French economist Thomas Piketty warned the world about the growing inequality, and his book published in 2014 became a best-seller in France and Japan.[9] The Japanese media reported that Carlos Ghosn, who was also the CEO of the French automobile manufacturer Renault, had an intention to avoid criticisms by the French directed toward his extremely high income. The figures are convincing. If this is true, that he underreported his compensation simply because he did not want to aggravate the French mentality, it would be a case of human sentimentality skewing the judgment of this internationally acclaimed businessman.

The introductory textbooks of economics postulate that people are not concerned about other people's interests. In other words, people are purely self-interested. One might concede to this idea thinking there are so many self-indulgent people in society, but perhaps even these people are looking at more successful people around them and feeling jealous deep down. Books Sanseido's Shin Meikai kokugo jiten (a dictionary

---

[7] Data is taken from the International Social Survey Programme 2009 Social Inequality IV.

[8] More on this topic can be found in Luttmer (2005).

[9] Piketty described the French society based on historical data as well as by drawing on narratives such as novels and short stories. See Piketty (2014) for more details.

of the Japanese language) defines *"ninjo"* to be "a mental disposition that all people are endowed with, which reveals their human side." Feeling a pang of jealousy can be a human nature, that is *"ninjo."* However, this humanity aspect of an individual may play a part in making a successful business. It is often said that it takes about 10 years of apprenticeship to become a seasoned sushi chef. Takafumi Horie, a famous Japanese entrepreneur, dismisses this cliche. He claims that one can become a professional sushi chef in a year if one has an acute sense of business and management skills. From the perspective of economics, this claim seems plausible. I therefore put this point to a friend who worked as a sushi chef in Paris. Agreeing with the entrepreneur's assertion to an extent, he replied:

> Technically, it would be possible if these conditions were met,

but he pointed out that there were two non-technical factors that were equally important. Firstly, it is the ability to ensure high quality ingredients. The quality of fish from the market cannot be predicted, so the sushi chef needs to find good quality fish on the spot and procure them as cheaply as possible. Some people may be good at spotting good quality fish without much experience, but the trouble is that suppliers do not always display the best products on their shelves. They reserve the very best fish for their favorite long-term customers. In other words, it owes to maintaining good connections with suppliers. Secondly, such chefs also need to be adept at the art of communication. This is particularly the case in well-established upmarket sushi restaurants that attract a clientele of certain social standings, those who have been socially successful and have rich life experience. They often like to talk to the chef who prepares sushi in front of them over the counter. It could be about anything from general topics about sushi to current affairs in society. The chef needs to discern, through his observation, who this distinguished-looking gentleman customer may be, and entertain him by amiably taking part in the conversation. Even with a familiar customer, the chef must know what kind of mood this regular customer may be in on this particular visit. With all these observation and entertainment going on, he concentrates on making his work of art—sushi. It takes a multi-tasking person to successfully provide both good food and an enjoyable, entertaining time, just like a magician. A seasoned sushi chef is therefore someone who has mastered all these skills on top of the art of the traditional culinary endeavor while being an expert in sentimental empathy, backed by his/her life experience. Now, back to the original proposition, could a young chef in his 20s meaningfully entertain an epicurean gentleman customer in his 50s? Thus, my friend concludes:

> So, it would take about 10 years after all even if the man was talented.

As long as market participants are humans, there will be a hidden dynamism in operation, which cannot be explained by the introductory economics textbooks. The economy in the real world is far more complex, and one needs to understand what human sentiments do to it. A "seasoned" economist must be able to probe this aspect

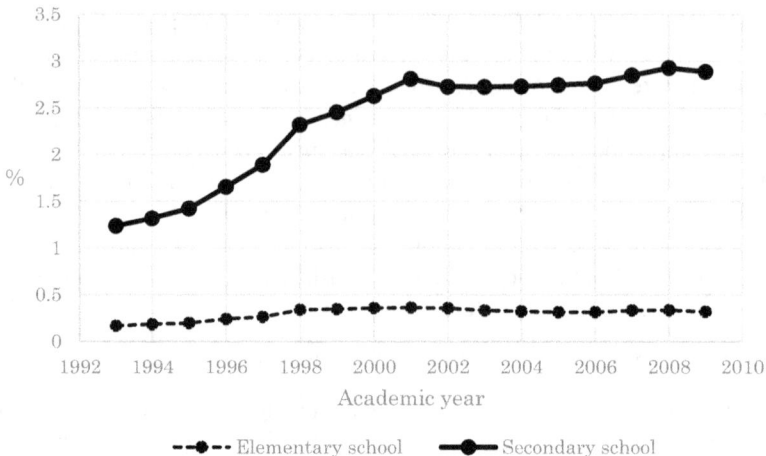

Fig. 3.1 Trend of chronic absence

in depth.[10] Having made an ostentatious point, I wonder if I am one. I put this to the readers to decide. Let me introduce some interesting topics for your judgment.

What Does Adam Smith Have in Common with an Old Lollipop Man?

I walk to my workplace, Seinan Gakuin University. It takes about 20 min. Passing through a bridge over the Muromi river, I throw a glance at the Hakata Bay in the downstream. A gust of wind catches my flat cap, so I turn it around to position the visor behind my neck, like a baseball catcher does. It saves me from having the cap blown off my head. Moving on, some landmarks appear to the left from the Yokatopia-dori Avenue, such as the Fukuoka Tower and Fukuoka City Museum. Turn to the right, there is Seinan Gakuin University. Nishijin Elementary School stands adjacent to it. I see its pupils pass in front of the university every day. Now, the road is relatively busy with people and traffic, but there is a junction without traffic lights. And there, an old man voluntarily appears day in day out, with a "safe traffic" flag in his right hand. He greets every passer-by with his "good morning." He advises school pupils to be mindful of the traffic, lowering his eye level to theirs. He is always there, rain or shine. His gaze at these children is as gentle as if admiring some treasure. He greets me, and I reciprocate. Thus starts my day.

Fostering trust in people can be catalytic for economic developments. As indicated in Fig. 3.1, there was a rise in the truancy of longer than 30 days among students

---

[10] This is my personal opinion. There are no established definitions about what a "seasoned economist" entails.

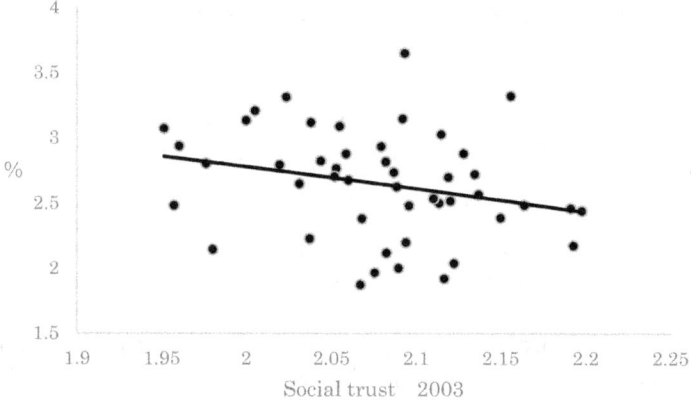

Fig. 3.2 Mapping of social trust and chronic absence at secondary schools

in the late 1990s. In particular, the figures for secondary-school students (aged 13 to 15) doubled in year 2000, from 1.2% in 1992. The thirty-year period leading up to today is characterized by the palpable social problem of so-called NEET and the reclusive individuals among young generations. The rising trend of chronic absenteeism among secondary-school students corresponds to the growing number of such individuals. Fostering trust in local communities might help children at elementary and secondary schools to strengthen their ties with society. It might throw a light on possible solutions to the NEET problem. With this idea in mind, I analyzed the impact of social trust on the chronically truant students at elementary and secondary schools, using 2004 data concerning the Japanese population.[11]

Figure 3.2 illustrates that stronger social trust corresponds to lower incidence of truancy among secondary school students. The same trend was observed for elementary school children, though it is omitted in the chart.

Low levels of truancy mean better learning environments. Social trust may enhance public education, which constitutes a part of the life in local communities. To assess this hypothesis, I conducted an additional analysis. The results revealed that stronger social trust was associated with higher scores of educational attainment among elementary-school students.[12] This finding implies that the community efforts to safeguard children foster relationships between them and local communities, so that they do not feel lonely, and they perform better at school.

It sometimes occurs to me while being preoccupied with my research, "why did Dr. Hayami agree to be my supervisor?" I visualize him, asking me "What contributions are you proposing to make?" I imagine that I represented a return of almost zero to his cost of providing me with supervision. Then why? Probably, it was the empathic disposition of an eminent economist that made him create an economist out of me.

---

[11] Yamamura (2011b).

[12] Yamamura (2012b).

What Comes Out from Mixing the Rich and the Poor?

A famous cat specialist, Akihiro Yamane, is a colleague of mine at Seinan Gakuin University. Being on a small campus, I see him on various occasions. One day, we were sitting together after lunch. I put to him a question.

> A tiger and a lion, which is stronger?

Both animals belong to the family of Felidae, which is why they are called big cats. In which case, I thought, cat specialists might already know the answer.

He replies, "That's an interesting question. Of course, it is unlikely that they meet in a fighting situation because they live so far away from each other. But if they did, the tiger might have an advantage by being able to climb up a tree. So, I think that the tiger will win."

As an inquisitive researcher, I offered a counterargument:

> I see, perhaps that is the case in a one-on-one battle. How about if it was a group fight, each having several individuals? Imagine a team sport, as opposed to individual sports. Lions hunt in groups, organized and coordinated to encircle and take down the prey. I saw it on YouTube. Tigers, on the other hand, they are loners, not team players."

He agrees, "That's true. In groups, perhaps, lions have the upper hand.

I continue, "If that's the case, it is possible to characterize them by their behavioral principles, that tigers are individualists like Westerners while lions are collectivists like the Japanese. We can then understand tigers like we understand Westerners, and lions like one of us."

I digressed a little from my initial question to expound a bizarre hypothesis that came off the top of my head. His response was impressive. He said,

> We need to contextualize them before coming to this conclusion. The environmental setups have to be taken into account in order to explain felids' behavioral principles. Tigers' habitats are found in Asian forests. They have learned to climb trees in order to sneak up on their prey without being noticed. Then, they have mastered their leaping attack, that requires the three-axis orientation. It's like Tiger Mask the wrestler from the 1980s, whose signature move was just like that. Meanwhile, lions live on the plains of the African savanna, where they have hardly a chance to hide. It is therefore very difficult to hunt individually as prey is more likely to spot them and run away. In order to survive, lions had to learn to hunt in groups.

The cat expert's wealth of knowledge and insightfulness were overwhelming. The same approach is applied to human beings, that there are hunter-gatherers and agrarians, that evolved out of the environmental conditions of their habitats. Hunter-gatherers behave like tigers and agrarians like lions. They develop their unique cultures and follow unique paths of history. The Japanese are agrarians by nature, to whom coordinated team play is vital in community life. This provided a ground for feudal relationships to develop, and in such relationships, sense of obligation and compassion was highly valuable.[13] While this could be a portrayal of typical Japanese

---

[13] Hayami (2000: Chap. 9).

persona of the past, the question is, would this apply to the modern Japanese population? Furthermore, supposing that there is an element of the sense of obligation and compassion as prerequisite of interpersonal relationships in Japan, what implications can be found from the perspective of economics?

Too great the income disparity in a group does create uneasiness between people. It is only a natural reaction to feel envious and jealous towards one who comes dressed in luxury clothes that you cannot afford. It is what human sentiment does to you. Then, it suggests that cooperative relationships between the rich and the poor would be a difficult task to accomplish. Economics in its classical form presupposes individuals who act solely on their own interest. This precludes the problem of feeling jealous towards others on account of their sentiments. Supposing that jealous sentiments are at play with these individuals, still the problem would not arise if the high earners were grouped together among themselves and never mix with a group of low-income people. This would be the case of the social class system that developed in Europe to create a stable society and bring it to maturity. Over there in Europe, great value is placed on modern individualism, having evolved through history. Though to different degrees, their economy focuses on individuals more than on organizations. By contrast, Japan has been growing its economy through the power of organizations. Since its modernization in the late nineteenth century, Japan has seen no fixed social class system in operation, and people from different walks of life form organizations to pursue common interest. To put it broadly, Japan's economic growth was backed by the mechanism that functioned on the basis of obligation and comradery sentiments, typical of Asian communities. Even in modern Japan, there are neighborhood community organizations that encourage local residents to socialize with one another. You find them in urban Tokyo, too, organizing such events as summer parties and *mikoshi* float parades for the locals. With all these community activities making occasions for people to mix with others, the income disparity must certainly get in their way. Inspired by this notion, I conducted a statistical analysis.[14]

I collected statistical data on the Japanese population at the individual level for the following information: an opinion score as a variable, based on a scale on which greater values are accorded to the responses of stronger agreement with a statement, "the government should minimize the economic inequality in society"; respondents' prefecture of residence; and their household incomes. I also used the data taken by the NHK about how frequently people took part in neighborhood community organizations, which were organized by respondents' prefectures of residence. The data was merged with the individual data according to their prefectures of residence, with which I quantified the socialization among community members in the places they lived. The outcomes of the calculation based on this set of data were as follows:

(1) the higher the frequency of socialization in a community, the more likely that high-income members agree with the idea of wealth redistribution by the government, and

---

[14] Yamamura (2012a).

(2) low-income members of the community generally agree with the idea of wealth redistribution by the government, but the extent of their agreement does not correspond to the frequency of their community socialization.

These may be interpreted that community socialization increases a chance of a high-income group meeting worse-off people and necessarily feel that the government has to minimize the income disparity in order to remove emotional barriers between people and to uplift the levels of satisfaction about their own lives. Meanwhile, a low-income group wants wealth redistribution under the government's initiative, which would bring them financial benefits, but this is not affected by whom they socialize with. In this way, organized community socialization generates an incentive for the wealthy segment of the population to consider their worse-off counterparts.

In summer, the NHK Radio 1 broadcasts a special program, the Children's Telephone Science Clinic in Summer Vacation, aired in the morning during the school holiday period. This is a live program, in which about three specialists, representing different fields of interest every day, answer the questions posed by school children who phone in. There is one particular specialist who tickles my imagination as he always so passionately discusses his subject matter with the child who has a question for him. This is Professor Yoshitsugu Kobayasi, a dinosaur expert at Hokkaido University. One day, a schoolboy named Eisuke came with a question, "which is stronger, a T-Rex or Spinosaurus?" An enthusiastic discussion took place between the professor and the boy. It was just like the conversation I had with Professor Yamane, as described at the beginning of this section. I sometimes recall vividly the memory of the mixed martial arts fight between Antonio Inoki and Muhammad Ali, that took place in 1976. I was merely seven or eight years old. Before the fighters entered the ring, there was an announcement, in an excited voice, that the match was broadcast live to dozens of countries via satellite. I remember the enthusiastic mood emanating in the venue, people cheering their favorite contestant as they made an entry. I remember the exaltation, the thrill, and the anticipation of a spectacular fight to unfold. I remember how Antonio Inoki rolled out his secret move. As I remember all these, that moment I am back in time—a little schoolboy who contemplates on his signature move.

What Can We Learn from the Life of Kazuo Ishiguro About Government Finance?

> I trusted. I trusted in his lordship's wisdom. All those years I served him, I trusted that I was doing something worthwhile. I can't even say I made my own mistakes.

A lead character of the story, an old butler, confesses with tears in his eyes. This is a line from the last scenes of *The Remains of the Day*, a masterpiece of Kazuo Ishiguro, a British author who was awarded the Nobel Prize in Literature in 2017. The butler dedicated his life to the loyal service of Lord Darlington, an influential figure in British international diplomacy during the war period. His master, to whom he placed unquestioning fealty, ends up being subjected to social condemnation, his prestigious standing destroyed. The loyal butler, despite his unshakable allegiance to his Lordship, finally acknowledges the mistake his master made in his life. This is a powerful, emotionally-charged scene. Ishiguro's characters in different works share something in common. They are described in a contrast between their memories of past glory and the present that is marked with a tarnished reputation. For example, his *An Artist of the Floating World* features a legendary painter whose successful life comes to an end as he is charged, in a post-war inquisition, with the crime of being a painter of imperial appointment to promote the war. As a Japan-born British, Ishiguro has two relationships with his country of origin. One is with Japan in his remote memories, and the other is with the modern Japan that is distant in space. Thus, he must have a vantage point from which he observes the discrepancies attributed to the lives of people who lived in these two "Japans." He then devises various plots that portray individuals who are confronted with the gap between how they remember their past and what they perceive the present to be.

The Japanese national budget for 2019 amounted to over 100 trillion yen for the first time in six years. Of the entire budget, more than 60% is accounted for by the state deficit (debt-servicing cost) and social security cost. According to the media report, "this is analogous to the 1940 budget, which earmarked two-thirds for the national defense budget and state bonds in the wake of the Pacific War. One could say, at the risk of misinterpretation, that the country is on the verge of a war on social security policies."[15] In summer 1941, a researcher of the Cabinet Research Institute for Total Warfare produced a detailed report on the prospect of the imminent battle based on objective data. It stated that Japan would be defeated if it went into a war with America. Despite the report, the government of the time decided to declare war, and consequently, Japan was defeated, as the report predicted.[16] Going to war disregarding the research institute's prospect report was a decision made on the judgment skewed by the political dynamics that prevailed in the government. A parallel may be drawn in the policy-making concerning the current affairs of national finance. The bill to increase the consumption tax is continually deferred, and matters of financial and structural reform are left untouched. It is incredible that politicians still believe in the plausibility of government-led economic growth. Meanwhile, Japan remains devoid of policies that the country needs for a truly sustainable future.

An era is coming to a close as Japan anticipates the instatement of a new emperor. The country has come a long way to enjoy material prosperity and embrace human rights in respect of the dignity of the individual, even though some issues remain. These are positive aspects of Japan, in my opinion. The problem is that it is almost impossible to grow economically as it has done in the past. A success story from the 70s and 80s is no longer relevant. "Acceleration of growth" cannot realistically be expected. The government strategies for growth, formulated regardless, would be fruitless. This is because the social and economic conditions are completely different

---

[15] Shimazawa (2019).

[16] Inose (2010).

from those half a century ago. The lexicon of Generation Z illustrates this. In the modern age when smartphones are the norm, the young generation calls a good-old feature phone "Gala-cellphone," implying the Galapagos Islands, where biological evolution took a remarkably different course from the rest of the world. In an analogy, perhaps, proponents of economic policies that are based on the legend of glorious economic growth from many decades ago must be termed as "Galapagos economists," whose idea of economy is irrelevant to the present world.

A more pressing issue is that, for the sake of an immediate economic boost, the government heavily relies on issuing bonds. As enduring and reliable economic growth cannot be guaranteed, the government deficit is passed on to our children and their children. It is a scheme that benefits the current generations and deprives the future ones, that protects the standard of life for those who are alive today but takes away a chance of living from those who are yet to be born. A pragmatic solution would be to distribute the burden across generations. In this sense, raising the rates of consumption tax would be inevitable, and yet the political parties of today are adamantly opposed to this. The reason is obvious: politicians need votes to be elected before they realize the policies they promise, and supporting the tax hike is a popularity liability in the face of tax-paying voters. This is a simple demand–supply equation. If there is a growing demand for policies that take into account the interest of future generations, politicians will change their tune in what they propose.[17] This being said, it is generally agreed that people draw on their past experiences to determine their actions. An empirical study of economics reveals that the financial circumstances experienced during the period of adolescence are a determinant factor of the standard values of people in their adulthood.[18] What can be done to overcome this aspect of human nature? The clue is to place ourselves in an extended time spectrum.

The fundamental difficulty in addressing Japan's fiscal problem is found in the fact that the existing political and economic systems are forced onto the problem unprecedented in human history. To explain this, I refer to the argument advanced by a professor at Keio University, Keiichiro Kobayashi, who takes an approach

---

[17] The so-called "new generation" of the post-modernization Japan, those who comprise the major social drive today, seem to be blindfolded by the "bubble economy" which the country enjoyed in the 1980s to early 1990s. This is the generation that only knew Japan as a reasonably prosperous country, boasting its economic power and promising future growth. For these people, the rigid social system is tolerable because it offers a life-long security by assimilating into it at the cost of somewhat restrained personal freedom. When still young, their primary concern was how to lead a meaningful, humane life, betting on the promise of economic growth. They chose to make a living out of insecure "part-time" jobs, and spent their free time in search of the ways to make their dreams come true. This illustrates a typical pattern based on their values. I am one of them, and I chose not to waste my life by fitting in a corporate machine. Instead, I spent a few years backpacking the world to witness the reality. When I speak with people of my generation, in our 50s, I sometimes come under the impression that some of us still live in the illusion of the past. By contrast, my students live in the real world of today. To their eyes, our "new generation" people may be appearing as living fossils.

[18] Giuliano and Spilimbergo (2014).

which integrates political philosophy and market economy.[19] The democracy that was developed from the premodern through to the modern era in Japan, is a participatory decision making system, which accords everyone an equal right to participate. There, the participants both enjoy its benefits and bear the cost. Participants of the future may express their opinions as agents unrelated to past events. As decisions are made repeatedly through the democratic process, the best interest of the majority is reflected in policies at any given time. This system is built upon the efforts of relevant parties to seek the best decisions for their interest. This is a liberal way of thinking in the sense that it severs the time continuity from the past to the present. Keeping the past conditions in mind to make decisions, in other words, taking the passage of time into consideration, is regarded a conservative ideology. The difference between the two is in whether the past is taken into the equation to consider problems of the present. However, decision-making for current affairs without considering the flow of time leads to tragic consequences not in the present, but in the future. Then, this chain of thoughts leads us to realize that there is a limit to the pursuit of personal interest by individual free agents.

Let us consider the role of "sympathy," as propounded by Adam Smith, as in assuming other people's points of view.[20] In a community, sympathy was an important factor for people coming face to face with one another. However, there was a need to establish a rule-based market that extended beyond the community boundary in order to solve the poverty in society at large. This led to the establishment of tacit collaborative relationships.[21] The market functions by means of individuals, alive at present, seeking their own interest. Social security is provided by the government, as the market cannot cover it. The cost required for the social security will be paid for from taxes or state debt (government bonds). Then, government spending and who bares the cost are determined indirectly by the public. In other words, all voters can take part in this decision-making. However, the decision will not reflect the interest of those who are excluded from this process, namely, the under-age population and unborn future generations. Thus, generational disparity keeps growing. What the country needs now is the timeless sympathy between generations. More specifically, it is the ability of their generation of the present world to sympathize with future generations and understand their interest with substantial conviction, as the latter does not have the advantage to express their own interest. Then, a group has to be formed by some members of the living generation to totally sympathize with the future generations and represent their interest to influence the decision-making on policies. In this way, we will be able to make arrangements for striking a balance between the interest of different generations and further develop a sustainable economy. An idea as far-fetched as this may seem only possible in science fiction, but miracles can happen, as we have seen in Chap. 1, the in-street mime artists of the city of Bogota. It is possible to build a new system paying due attention to the temporal continuity, then

---

[19] Kobayashi (2018).

[20] Studies by Adam Smith offer us significant insights into some research topics for advanced areas such as behavioral economics and brain science (Doume 2008: Afterword).

[21] Kandori (2014).

past and future become relevant. We, the generation of here and now, are responsible for making society sustainable.

As Kobayashi points out, liberal thinking tends to disregard the time spectrum while conservative ideologies are likely to value temporal continuity. In Japanese politics, however, the continuity is undervalued not only by opposition parties, but also by the conservative, governing parties. The latter takes into account the section of time trajectory between the past and the present, but further ahead to the future they do not. They ignore considerably reliable predictions based on objective facts, and in this, they resemble the Cabinet Office of pre-war Japan. Kazuo Ishiguro writes futuristic stories, too. Imagine, a novel by him, set in future Japan. It may feature people who struggle in the gap between the past and the present, where the past Japan in their memories would be today, the present for us. The main character may be a key person in financial policy making… Who knows? Would he be interested in this idea of mine to write a new novel?

Municipalities That Fared Well in the Tax-Deductible Donation Scheme by Not Offering Thank-You Gifts[22]

The government introduced a new tax-deductible donation program, called "Furusato Nozei," or hometown tax donation scheme in 2008. It has been more than 10 years since its launch, and the tax-deductible donations to municipalities rocketed a staggering 40-fold. Ironically, the progressive expansion of the scheme seems to drive it away from its main purpose. That is, the government has repeatedly requested local governments to "limit the values of gratuitous goods below 30% of the donations received," but as many as 116 municipalities, as of November 2018, disregard this request and offer more valuable items as thank-you gifts. One such case is the municipality of Oyama in Shizuoka prefecture. The Oyama administration decided just after the government issued the request to add to their offerings shopping vouchers worth 40% of the donated amount. The result was 25 billion yen in donation through this scheme, 9 times over on the previous fiscal year. The town mayor was reported to have confided that he "made the decision out of desperation" given the critically tight municipal finance, being fully aware of the main purpose of the scheme.[23] This case suggests that the hometown tax donation scheme cannot rely on the discretion and prudence of local authorities. After this incident, the government reviewed and amended the program in June 2019, according to which Oyama and three other municipalities were removed from the scheme.

The Furusato Nozei scheme is designed to appeal to tax-payers by drawing on the sentimental attachment to their hometowns. It was regarded as an innovative

---

[22] The main part of this section is taken from Yamamura (2018), with some additions and modifications.

[23] *The Nihon Keizai Shimbun*, February 4, 2019: 27.

economic experiment by the government, and yet it will be remembered as a catastrophic failure in modern history. The question is, how did it happen that the reality of the scheme diverged from its intended cause? We will dissect this problem from the perspective of behavioral economics, taking people's "psychological habits" into account.

To start with, let me describe the background and the scheme's cause. On June 1, 2007, the Ministry of Internal Affairs and Communications called the first meeting of experts, forming a working group to develop a program to facilitate tax-deductible donations to municipalities. Named the Hometown Revenue Contribution Scheme Working Group, this initiative aimed "to implement regulatory measures of taxation that enable tax-payers to make contributions to their hometowns … inspired by the desire of tax-payers who live and work away from the places where they were born and brought up." This initiative is a response to the awareness of a growing disparity in tax revenue between regional areas, where the working population continues to diminish, and urban areas, which prosper by virtue of the labor migration from poorer regions. It was necessary to alleviate the growing inequality, which led to the introduction of the tax-deductible donation scheme, Furusato Nozei. One thing they did not foresee was the extent to which the scheme proved to have an impact on tax redistribution: the meeting minutes of the second Hometown Revenue Contribution Scheme Working Group states that "the Furusato Nozei scheme may not grow sufficiently to have a direct impact on the disparity in tax revenue distribution, but some indirect contributions can be expected." In reality, however, diminished tax revenues of major cities have become a palpable problem in the last few years, attributed to the revenue redistribution through the scheme. Then the question is, what exactly was going on?

A review of the rules and issues of the scheme is in order. This scheme allows tax-payers to choose the municipalities in which they do not live to give donations to, and a proportion of the paid amount will be deducted, with some restrictions, from the local income tax to be paid to their own local authorities. In this way, it has an effect of rearranging the distribution of tax revenues among local authorities. Therefore, reduced tax revenue in urban areas is anticipated to an extent as the local taxpayers redirect their money to local governments in regional areas. This in itself is within the cause of the scheme. The problem lies in the following two rules: (1) tax-payers may choose the target municipality arbitrarily except the one in which they reside, and (2) the beneficiary government may offer goods in return as a token of gratitude. While the scheme is based on the principal idea of making financial contributions to the municipal government of one's hometown, Rule 1 allows a very liberal notion of a "hometown," including the municipalities that have nothing to do with participating tax-payers. This is perhaps because a system to verify the donor's relation to the beneficiary municipality would cost extremely high, making this unfeasible. Rule 2 gives tax-payers an incentive to participate in the scheme, but such participation would be based on the want of a material return. To illustrate this simply (though in reality it is more complex and with some constraints), imagine, you donate 5,000 yen through this scheme and receive a gift that is worth 2,000 yen in market value. You would have lost the 5,000 yen in local income tax anyway, so

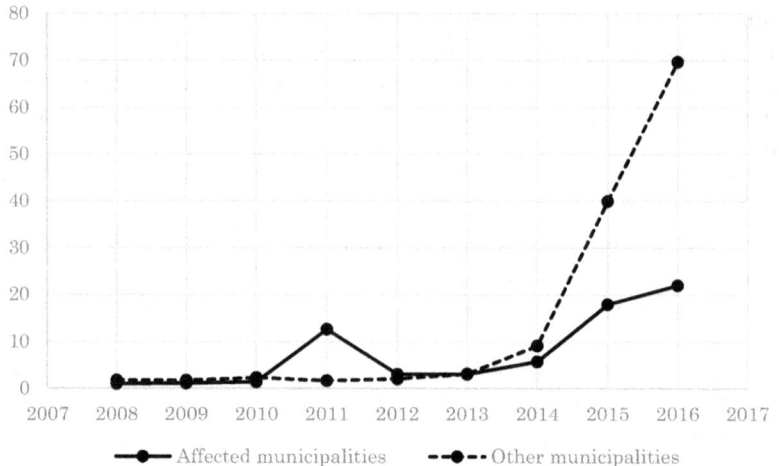

Fig. 3.3 Tax-deductible donation to municipalities in value compared between the municipalities that suffered in the 2011 major earthquake disaster and the others. *Source* Data available on the Ministry of Internal Affairs and Communications official website. *Note* The perpendicular axis is for collected donations converted into index numbers against the base number of 100 based on the 2008 value for the local authorities of affected municipalities

it amounts to paying tax and simply getting a free gift worth 2,000 yen. This means that, Rules 1 and 2 combined, the scheme may incentivize people to use it in order to gain cost-free goods, and the sentimental attachment to their hometowns will be completely irrelevant. Then, it is only natural that tax-payers are inclined to choose the municipality that offers the highest-value goods in return.

The 2011 major earthquake was one of the most significant events that happened to Japan after the introduction of this tax donation scheme. While previous research has already identified the positive correlation between the degree of trust and sense of contentment among people, a joint research I conducted has suggested that this correlation is stronger after the earthquake disaster than before the event. There is also a study that illustrates how participation in volunteer work increased after the 1996 Kobe earthquake and how this tendency was clearer in areas closer to the stricken regions. These suggest that natural disasters stimulate people's bonds of trust and prompt them to engage in acts of altruism. I analyzed the donations collected by local authorities in the Furusato Nozei scheme, using the data from my joint research.[24] Figure 3.3 illustrates the trends of the average amounts collected by the earthquake-stricken local authorities and those by all the other local governments. The donation is on an increase overall, and particularly remarkable after 2013. It should be noted that donations to earthquake-stricken municipalities were temporarily boosted in 2011, but the same trend is not observed for the rest of the country. This suggests the underlying altruistic motive to give support to the people in those areas. A further in-depth analysis yielded the following findings: (1) the

---

[24] Yamamura et al. (2021).

municipalities offering gratuitous goods of higher values attract more donations, and (2) there are individuals who choose to give donations to the municipalities that offer no gifts in return, but if these local authorities change their policies and introduce thank-you gifts, their donation revenues will shrink almost to a quarter. This adverse effect of introducing a return gift policy was particularly noticeable with the local authorities in earthquake-stricken areas. This is interpreted that people who were using the scheme with their altruistic motives lost their sense of purpose when they were offered a material return. In other words, the rule that promotes self-interested motives discourages people with altruistic motives. And finally, (3) thank-you gifts have a greater impact on the amount of donation collected in case (1) above than in case (2). In general, however, offering gratuitous goods in return boosts revenues in donation.

Professor Uri Gneezy of the University of California San Diego has done interesting research on the behavior of parents who come to pick up their children at daycare centers.[25] Some daycare centers introduced a financial penalty applicable to parents who fail to pick up their children on time. As a result, parents' tardiness increased. Gneezy analyzes as follows: the parents were feeling guilty for not showing up on time, but the introduction of a financial penalty justified the tardiness, lifting the sense of guilt for not respecting the pick-up schedule. In other words, a system that was previously functioning well by virtue of rule-abiding people's moral sense became dysfunctional due to the introduction of a factor based on economic trade. When they withdrew the fine to rectify the situation, it worsened. There was nothing to stop the parents from being late when the penalty incentive was removed after corrupting their moral sense and respect for rules. It is not easy to restore moral standards once destroyed.

The Japanese government amended the Local Tax Act in March 2019, specifying that the values of gifts-in-return "should be no more than 30% of the amounts donated." This amendment will be enforced in June 2020. This change will formalize the gratuitous goods and their upper limit values, and by recognizing what has hitherto kept ambivalent as an explicit rule, there is a chance that people's moral sense and incentive to abide by the rules will be lost, just like the parents in the daycare center study. It will probably be the case that, with the "upper limit of the free gift value" rule in place, the local authorities which respected the cause of the tax-deductible donation scheme and did not offer any gratuitous goods before will introduce their free gifts. I think the government should prohibit the gifts altogether before spoiling people's moral standards. It may significantly diminish the overall donations, but at least the scheme will be able to achieve its true cause as participating donors will be genuine in their act of altruism.

---

[25] Gneezy and List (2014: Chap. 1).

How Can Takarasiennes Always Maintain Their Modesty, Fairness, and Graceful Beauty?—The Reason for the Unwaning Popularity of the Takarazuka Revue Company

The stage hits the climax, and Rio Asumi, a top star actress playing a male role, steps off the stage toward the audience, walks past my aisle-side seat and takes a seat a few rows behind me, her legs crossed and one arm resting on the shoulders of a female audience next to her, all the time singing. Her smile and a little wink at the audience stir up a fanatic sensation. This was my first ever experience of the Takarazuka Revue performance in live. The troupe was touring in Fukuoka, and a friend of mine gave me a couple of tickets, which certainly was hard to come by otherwise. Apparently, this friend has a daughter who performs in the company.

The show was impressive, so much so that I kept singing the songs featured in the production in my head, going over and over again the refrains, until the next day. Looking back, I had a premium seat that came with the privilege of seeing top stars up close. The Takarazuka Revue is a famous all-female stage performance company, so some performers play male parts, singing and dancing with a fake mustache and so on. The majority of the audience is women. My wife, who accompanied me to the show, says that the Takarazuka version of men are truly ideal men from female points of view, while men in the real world cannot be perfect no matter how good-looking they may be. Men played by women, who have a perfect understanding of how they idealize men, manifest faultless personification of this gender, superseding the men in reality. What an insightful story…

My friend's daughter performed a female part. Her stage name is Urara Haruhi. I received a letter, following the tickets, hand-written by the actress, describing her character in the program and detailing her appearances on stage. There were about 10 bird-eye-view drawings of the stage, each indicating where she would be positioned among all other actresses. She also wrote descriptions of each scene. When you are a top star, everyone would easily spot you on stage, but when you are not, it is vital to inform your fans in advance so that they can identify you among the entourage. For performers of the Takarazuka Revue Company, it is not all about singing, dancing, and acting. It is part of their job to write letters to their fans and devotees, providing information and thanking for their support. Adding to these efforts, there are parents who play an important role in promoting their daughters to friends and acquaintances. Their efforts to sell tickets are voluntary, on the basis of which there develops a network of cost-free sales agents. People who buy tickets through this network become fans of particular performers, who are daughters of someone they know. In this way, actresses, being top stars or otherwise, build up a cluster of avid followers and devotees. It is a whole package of these unsung efforts that support the dazzling and exuberant stages of the Takarazuka Revue. The performers express their gratitude to and appreciation of their fans through the show, and the fans appreciate it.

In the theater, it is almost impossible to identify who is who though each performer must be unique and talented in their own rights. If there were no possibilities to buy tickets through personal connections, people would favor top stars, who are easily identified. It would be difficult for non-top-star members of the company to create their fanbases. In terms of economics, also, it would be an ideal situation if people bought their tickets knowing every member of the cast every time, but this is not the case in reality. This is why it is so valuable that parents and other relatives or close friends of performers play a part in ticket sales on their behalf. In this endeavor, it is not closely-tied, long-standing relationships, but light and wide-spread connections of people that is fundamental. In his *The Strength of Weak Ties*, Mark Granovetter makes the following assertion: when people are in search of jobs, it is not the strong ties within an exclusive community but the weak ties of an open society that are advantageous.[26] For example, if you have many acquaintances that you meet only occasionally to chat with, you are more likely to come across information about workplaces looking for employees. People would have a degree of empathy with others when they personally circulate information about job opportunities.

Parental love is an essential part of the Takarazuka Revue Company. Only one in twenty-five is admitted to the Takarazuka Music School, a prerequisite for full membership of the revue. Top stars are nominated among the peers, then their status is fixed—no one will replace them until the top-stardom is passed on to the next generation. No matter how many fans they gain, the entourage actresses will never step into the limelight. Their parents do their best behind the scenes, so that their pride and joy will be blessed with the popularity they deserve.

How Does Ninjo (Human Sentiments) Enrich the Market Economy?

Standard economics focused on market economy considers that a society will become materially prosperous by virtue of individuals solely pursuing their own interest. One of the shortcomings of the market economy is that it is not equipped to stop the growing disparity. Meanwhile, opponents of market economy, such as communism and socialism, used to be considered as powerful alternatives, but nations that allowed the government authorities to manage their economy followed a path to tragic consequences. This is called a "government failure" in economics. How about a society that is based on a "community," as we have seen earlier. Without going into details, I will mention one such society, which went to a total denial of elitism and affluence in order to revive a primitive community: this is Cambodia under the Pol Pot regime, which eventually amounted to nothing but tragedy and confusion. Human history eloquently tells us that economy left to the hands of a government or community only had futile results. By the turn of the century, market economy was the one that survived. It comes with disparities, but these are temporary ones, never

---

[26] It is known that weak personal ties are viable when looking for jobs (Granovetter 1973).

permanent. In a long-term perspective, descendants of the rich may end up belonging to a low-income segment of the population, or vice-versa. Those who believe in the "American dream" enabled by working hard to strike gold in the market economy stick to their self-help efforts without counting on government support. This ideology was expounded in logical terms by a French economist, Thomas Piketty. Come the twenty-first century, this idea was verified anew based on historical data, casting a light on the fact that market economy engendered a disparity that kept growing over a long period.[27] Ironically, it was Piketty who found it.[28] State, community, and market, all these types of economy come with their issues. In my opinion, the fundamental problem is found in the manner in which they ignored human sentiments and sympathy and applied ivory tower theorizing to a real world system. What, then, would the economic system that is accounted for by human sentiments look like?

Let us take Professor Kandori's arguments as a starting point. A market brings considerable satisfaction to society by allowing many unrelated individuals to participate.[29] It enables people to obtain goods that they could not procure from persons in their social circles. For example, for a Japanese person, he or she would not know personally anyone who cultivates good coffee beans. Even so, there are coffee aficionados in Japan, and those who are not one can also enjoy good coffee in cafes, etc. The coffee they consume comes from coffee-producing regions in other countries, cultivated by coffee farmers. The Japanese consumers are not acquainted with these farmers, but they can simply choose to drink coffee by paying the price for the commodity. By contrast, a community economy is sustained by dyadic relationships among community members. The group may be small in number, but it functions not on the basis of monetary incentives. There is a shared norm of helping others that is in operation in the community. Imagine Japanese society as a closed community, it is impossible to procure coffee beans through its exclusive interpersonal relationships. If someone gives you some coffee, it must have come from a certain foreign supplier.

Kandori argues that the result of abstracting the community economy and the norm of mutual help to a state level is a restrained society in which its inhabitants are under surveillance by other members. This society, he asserts, will be subject to a reign of terror by an autocratic dictator. There are cases that demonstrate his point. The socialist states that found themselves on the brink of collapsing around the year 2000. What came out of a revolution that pushed community rules to a national level? Abstract arguments aside, take a look at what happened in Ethiopia toward the end of the last century.

> At the beginning of the Revolution all of us had utterly rejected anything to do with the past. We would no longer drive cars, or wear suits; neckties were considered criminal. Anything that made you look well-off or bourgeois, anything that smacked of affluence or sophistication, was scorned as part of the old order. ... Gradually materialism became

---

[27] Piketty (1995).
[28] Piketty (2014).
[29] Kandori (2014).

Table 3.2 Patterns of economic development

	Social capital	Education of the management
Early stage (community rules)	Positive effect	Negative effect
Expansion stage (market rules)	Negative effect	Positive effect

accepted, then required. ... We had the best of everything: the best homes, the best cars, the best whiskey, champagne, food. It was a complete reversal of the ideals of the Revolution.[30]

The reason for the failure was because they did not take natural human desires into consideration. It is natural that people desire wealth and prosperity. It is part of the sentimental disposition human beings are endowed with. One could say that socialism saw its demise because it did not account for the human sentiments. However, does this signify that communities are insignificant to human society? I feel a pang of hesitation to agree with such a notion as this. What is wrong in extending a helping hand to community members who are right next to you? Isn't it possible that market economy also fails if it does not pay due attention to the human sentiments as an important factor? Unbeknownst to many, economists have been in search of a form that combines the advantages of both community and market economy. The gist of it is described as follows: while a society is still in a premature state without well-developed systems to support market trade, such as legal regulations, it relies on a community market model, ruled by norms and standards, but a community can only provide affluence to an extent, which necessitates a set of laws in order to expand market transactions and promote economic growth. In other words, it suggests a pattern of economic development that involves a transition from a community economy based on tacit rules to a market economy with formal systems and regulatory frameworks.[31]

I borrowed this framework of the evolution from community to market models and analyzed how Okayama prefecture developed an agglomeration of apparel industry, for which I conducted a fieldwork in the industrial complex of the Kojima area.[32] The data collected through the survey elucidated the patterns as illustrated in the Table 3.2. More specifically, I identified a structure that explained the development of the industrial agglomeration.

Let us assume that, in order to realize commercial growth, an apparel company needs a social reputation earned through years of operation and the management that is competent based on education. Call the former "the social capital of the company" and the latter "human capital of the management." Assume further that the management enhances its abilities by learning from actual management of the

---

[30] Acemoglu and Robinson (2013: 158).

[31] Hayami (2000).

[32] The Kojima area represents the country's largest cluster of school-uniform manufacturers, such as Kanko Gakuseifuku and Fuji Yacht, as well as major labels of jeans, like Big John. New high-end jeans brands have been created here in recent years (Yamamura 2009a).

company, and call this the "effect of learning." When the Kojima area was still in the early days of its industrial clustering, their businesses were rather confined in a small, closed community, governed by interpersonal relationships based on community rules (standards). Companies with larger "social capital" represent long-standing business relationships within the community. The company managers would have more opportunities to learn from their suppliers and clients, who are inside their social circles, and thus to enhance their companies' performance. It follows that the larger the social capital of the company, the greater the effect of learning for the management. Managers who had education in business management, however, are more likely to run their businesses to the rules of modern society rather than the inherent rules of the community. As these rules are incompatible, managers with greater degrees of human capital based on their education would act in violation of the community rules and be ostracized as a consequence. In such a case, educated managers would be deprived of meaningful opportunities to exercise their expertise as business managers.

When the agglomeration grows to a certain extent, market economy comes into play, requiring business managers to enrich their know-hows through a wide web of connections with trade partners outside the community boundary. In this situation, the educated managers have more advantages because they understand the rules shared in a wider arena of the business, gaining access to a greater effect of learning. It follows that the larger the human capital of the management, the greater the effect of learning for the management. By this stage, those managers who are partial to community rules will face difficulties in expanding their trade, being unable to understand how businesses work outside their community. As a result, the managers of companies with larger social capital would be more likely to miss profit-making opportunities.

My version of economic growth implies that an economy develops by establishing a set of universal rules that can operate globally while acknowledging the usefulness of the standards that should be respected among community members in order to sustain the economy. I have been contemplating on this world view for about a decade. It is applicable to economically developing societies with growing populations, such as that of Japan when it was undergoing rapid economic growth. However, our country today has evolved into a mature society with its legal and other social systems in place and its population rapidly aging. Any attempts to achieve economic growth will fail if they are modeled on past successful experiences. Japan needs to aspire to attain "small is beautiful," soft-landing on a sustainable society. A new set of prescriptions will be required if the modern Japanese society at the turn of the era is to grapple with the issues at hand. An emphasis should be placed on the subsidiarity between the "open community" and "market." This new type of community, supported by the sympathy that operates in organically-forming interpersonal relationships and open communication enabled by the Internet technology, would fill the gap left by the market.

There needs to be a type of trust that is nurtured by natural human affection, a bottom-up approach as opposed to a top-down, imposed sense of trust. The arts and culture have an indirect yet lasting power of influence over this natural human affection.[33] To bring this a step further, reconsider the role of a place to be shared with others. It is like the role played by the mime performers in the streets of the Columbian city of Bogota, mentioned in Chap. 1. The key notion that fills the gap between "market" and "sympathy" is hidden from the view of economists. This is a tough bunch, of course myself included, who demand tangible evidence in order to be convinced. However, as one says, "what is essential is invisible to the eye."[34] It is our duty as economists to probe what is invisible and visualize it. What we need in doing this is a type of sensitivity that has been quantified by means of a "love" hormone, oxytocin. It is a type of love innate in women.

---

[33] A pop-song in the early 1980s, *Some day*, by Motoharu Sano addresses disconnected young people, singing about the meaning of having a belief in others. This passionate, yet soft and melodic song is atypical of songs with political messages. It was my favorite when I was a student, whose impact may be lingering in my thinking today.

[34] Saint-Exupery (2006).

Chapter 4
What Will Become of Pupils in a Class with a Female Teacher?

In Chap. 2, I mentioned that, according to previous research in economics of education, the younger the children are, the greater the effect of education is, citing "Oshin" as an analogy.[1] Let us quickly recapitulate the gist: the children who had early education develop abilities not only in academic performance, but also in non-cognitive skills, such as perseverance and prosocial disposition. Given that the non-cognitive skills have implications to the values and perspectives the children develop later on, I wondered whether the genders of classroom teachers at elementary school had any impact in this matter. This idea set me out to gather data through my own survey and analyze the classroom teachers' impact on the value orientations of students.[2] In the survey, I reminded myself of the particular role of teachers in charge of Grade 1 classes for the following three reasons:

(1) just starting out in the school system, Grade 1 students are the most dependent on classroom teachers, and thus the most susceptible to their influence,
(2) classes are formed, and teachers are assigned, without external biases such as parents' express preferences of particular teachers or students' preferred choices, and
(3) matching of classes and teachers is arbitrary because schools have no prior information about new students to take their personality traits into consideration.

As a result, students are almost perfectly randomly assigned to a classroom and a teacher, irrespective of any bias from students, parents, or school administrators. This is an important factor. For example, a quiet child may prefer to be in a class with a female teacher because, in general, she would be gentle, or at last this would be the child's expectation. The school administration would prefer, or consider it appropriate, to put introvert children under the care of female teaching staff. Private schools may arrange an entry exam and pre-admission interviews with children's parents, where they can share information about the children's characteristics with

---

[1] Heckman (2015).
[2] Yamamura et al. (2019).

the administration and teachers. In this case, classes may be formed, and teachers assigned, with reference to the parents' input. Then, it is possible that children with a gentle temperament are likely to be in a class with a female teacher. This would pose a problem to my investigation because the children's 'gentle' nature is not a product of the female teacher but a trait already innate to them, and the supposed influence of the teacher is only "in disguise." This would hinder the evaluation of the influence exercised by female teachers. This idea led me to focus on state schools, which normally did not possess detailed information about children before they enter the school.

As I have already mentioned, gender difference has been scientifically verified in terms of cognition and behavior between men and women. Generally speaking, women are more socially aware than men. In other words, women are more likely than men to think and behave in terms not only of their personal interest, but also of the interest of society as a whole. To put this into context, think of the recent trend in the business world that companies should not only focus on making profits, but act responsibly in terms of the environment, communities, and correct governance.[3] The notion of acting in the diverse interest of society as a whole is represented by three keywords: environment, society, and governance, or ESG for short. The conjecture is that women are more aware of ESG. Adding to this, women produce more oxytocin than men do, as it has already been discussed in Chap. 1. This gives a basis to suppose that women are naturally or biologically predisposed to have higher ESG-awareness than men do. If this is the case, then the influence of female teachers may not be as great on girls as it is on boys. All these conjectures led to the following hypotheses:

> Hypothesis 1: being taught by a female teacher has little effect on girls in terms of their ESG-awareness in their adulthood.
>
> Hypothesis 2: being taught by a female teacher has an effect on boys in terms of their raised awareness of ESG in their adulthood.

To test these hypotheses, I included the following points in the survey: (a) their attitude to ESG,[4] and (b) the genders of their classroom teachers from Grades 1 to 6. The survey also asked the respondent's income level, employment status, and education levels of their parents, among other things. The analysis results indicated the following points:

---

[3] Byun and Oh (2018).

[4] The survey presented three statements and asked the respondents to indicate their responses on a scale of 1 (strongly disagree) to 5 (strongly agree).

The mean value of the three scores was used as the ESG-awareness variable. The statements are:

1. Business entities should make social contributions through their efforts in addressing environmental issues.

2. Business entities should contribute to society through initiatives for their local communities.

3. Business entities should ensure appropriate governance and transparency in their business management.

(1) women have higher ESG-awareness than men do,
(2) the influence of female teachers is not recognized in women who were taught by them,
(3) men who were taught by female classroom teachers at school grow up to become more aware of ESG, and
(4) the female teachers' influence is observed only when they teach Grade 1 classes.

Based on these outcomes, the hypotheses turned out to be approximately correct. The non-effect on girls suggests that female students already had the susceptibility to ESG at their schooling age. What interests me is that, overall, the values of female teachers are transmitted to young male students by virtue of spending much time together and influence their values though these boys are not old enough to even comprehend the concept of business entity. On this point, Simone de Beauvoir comes to my mind. She claimed that "one is not born, but rather becomes, a woman." How about men? We could say that one is not born, but becomes, a man. Take this as a hypothesis, the outcomes of the discussion hitherto support the first half, that one is born a man. However, whether one becomes a man seems to depend on the circumstances. If a boy grows up in close exposure to maternity, represented here by the female teachers, then he becomes a man with female gentleness, and if not, he develops into a "manly man." Progressive social empowerment of women increases the chance of boys spending more time with women in early stages of their personal development, and this may produce more "gentle-hearted men" in the future.

There is a story about a woman, a school teacher who followed up the lives of 12 individuals she taught as they were Grade 1 students. Many things happened to them in their lives: lives lost in the war, and one student lost his eyesight completely. A class reunion was organized, if incomplete with missing members. In the scene, the teacher calls the blinded man by his pet name. In her mind, the twelve students were as alive as they once had been. This story was adapted in a 1954 film, *The Twenty Four Eyes*, directed by Keisuke Kinoshita. The teacher was played by Hideko Takamine, whose performance was the Virgin Mary personified. The film is imbued with the affection between a teacher and her pupils, which is perhaps characterized by boys' eternal yearning for the grace of the Virgin Mary identified with their female teacher, and not the sort of infatuated affection with which schoolgirls look at their male teachers.

Women: Are They Born as Women or Do They Become Women?

I was in Paris in May 2018. This was the first time in some twenty years that I visited this city. The purpose of the visit was the conference of the Society of Economics of the Household (SEHO). There were some special lectures on the social participation for women, and one of lecturers was Raquel Fernández, a controversialist economist whose contention was that culture, including underlying values, undergo

Fig. 4.1 Photograph: a bookshop only a 10-min walk from Camus's apartment was having a special event on Simone de Beauvoir 2018 © Eiji Yamamura

transformation at the initiative of women.[5] I saw her sitting among the audience to a presentation being delivered by a young female researcher. Ms. Fernández was actively participating in the debate, and when the presenter commented that it would be difficult to realize what she suggested to her, this economist filled the venue with her sharp "We can do it!" then took a breath and once again, even louder than the first time. With her smart attire and gripping stare, she has a certain, powerful aura about her.

I listened to the special lecture, made my own presentation, then I took a liberty and left the conference. With a little drawing pad under my arm, I took a leisurely walk in the beautiful streets of Paris, making sketches from time to time. It suddenly occurred to me that Albert Camus had once lived near the metro station Saint-Sulpice, where his son still lived. I made my way to the address which I had heard from someone before. Arriving at an apartment building, I observed the labels on a panel of doorbells at the entrance and found "Camus" among them, handwritten indifferently.

In Paris, I am "l'étranger." As I continued toward the station, I suddenly got the feeling that someone was looking at me. A bookshop window came in my view. It was Simone de Beauvoir, sending out her calm yet telling gaze from inside the window. On a closer look, I found about a dozen books by or about her on display (Fig. 4.1). It looked like they were running a themed event on her.

A thought crossed my mind: her partner, the philosopher Jean-Paul Sartre and Camus used to be close friends, often entertaining passionate debates on existential questions, but eventually they fell out with each other. The year 2018 marked the 50th anniversary of May 68, an event in which Parisian students stirred a catastrophic civil

---

[5] See for example Fernandez et al. (2004).

unrest. It was also the 50th year since I was born. I imagine, Sartre and Beauvoir must have been seen among the crowd in protest. The riot still divides opinions. Nevertheless, 2018 was a significant benchmark for people of Paris. I let myself ponder—the president of France today was born after the national crisis, and perhaps the majority of residents in the city were born after the incident too… Then, my eyes caught sight of *The Second Sex*, Beauvoir's masterpiece text. It contains a famous passage:

> "One is not born, but rather becomes, a woman."

Posing a question to society, "is what makes a woman innate to her or is it molded on her as she grows up in society?" she created a sensational controversy in French society of her time. The book was published more than 50 years ago, but it still seems relevant today. The point she raised remained unresolved for a long time, partly because it depended on the points of view of people. Today, scientific approaches to human behavior have enabled empirical evaluation of the processes that generate gender differences. There are many economic researchers who, many of them being members of the Federation of Home Economics, proactively pursue relevant studies. The rest of this chapter is thus dedicated to some gender studies, through which we consider what may be expected out of the empowerment of women in society.

Women and Men, What Are the Differences?

My workplace, the Department of Economics at Seinan Gakuin University, has an academic credit system, according to which students are eligible for up to 2 credits by taking a tutorial in the fourth year. One credit is for taking the module, and the other is for submitting a successful dissertation. I make simple rules for my students: the credit for the module is awarded if the student took part in the tutorial and produced a 10-page final essay. For this essay, submission is sufficient to qualify, and the subject could be practically anything. As for the dissertation credit, it requires a longer essay, 16 pages minimum to be precise, of a satisfactory quality. For this quality requirement, I make suggestions for corrections or rewrites as many times as necessary. I tell the students who come to my tutorial that this option demands dedicated efforts because the expected quality level is very high. I say to them that enjoying research does not come by so easily and there is always hard work to be done, and give them a word of warning that they should not take this option unless they are ready to confront the hard work. I never coerce my students to write dissertations. If they decide to write one, however, I take their challenges seriously. If they give up half-way, that is their choice, and it is not my place to judge them. To those students who avoid dissertations and opt for final essays, I am an easy-going supervisor.

There are two types of students among those who decide to write dissertations under my supervision, knowing that it is destined be a thorny path. One is students who are genuinely interested in writing a dissertation, and the other is those who are compelled simply because they need this credit in order to compensate for the short total credit resulted from the previous three years of procrastination. The former causes almost no trouble for me, whereas the latter is almost always problematic—a submission deadline is not respected, and last-minute panic ensues. The majority of the latter group is male students. Female students are usually studious, writing up their dissertations well in time and to satisfactory quality levels. Some of them even try to improve their work after it is accepted to have met the quality requirement. There is another interesting phenomenon. With the final essays, I never return the manuscript for correction. The only requirement is the length of the essay. This being met, all they have to do is to submit it. From the standard economics point of view, this does not involve an incentive to write an essay of high quality. However, some students produce very good essays. They are as good as they could pass the quality mark for dissertations with a little improvement. Possible explanations are:

(1) they have friends who are working very hard on their dissertations and are inspired by their diligent attitude, so they make the same efforts to produce good quality pieces of writing,
(2) they are so intelligent that they weigh up the amount of effort required for a dissertation and decide to use the energy for more practical purposes (such as skill-based qualifications) instead, but with the intelligence they are able to produce good essays without much effort, or
(3) they overestimate the qualifying level of a dissertation and opt to be prudent, but such prudent students are often also attentive to whatever they do, and their attentiveness results in the raised quality of their essays.

The interesting part is that it is often female students who submit final essays of good qualities.

Take these three possible explanations as hypotheses, (3) seems most likely to explain the phenomenon concerning my tutorial students. This hypothesis is compatible with the knowledge of behavioral economics.[6] It tells us that women are less proactive than men in making a point or stating their opinions. They are not likely to run for an election unless they are absolutely confident of a victory. The axioms that explain the above are:

(1) women are strongly inclined to forgo risks, and
(2) men are more prone than women to unfounded certitude.

This point is explored in some biological studies. Oxytocin, as I have already mentioned in Chap. 1, is a biological substance associated with traits characteristic of females. It induces a sense of affection, sympathy, and happiness. A hormone that is often taken as its counterpart is testosterone, which is more associated with male characteristic traits. An increased level of testosterone makes one more aggressive and daring to confront risky situations. A study shows that, in a male derivatives trader, the testosterone levels rise after a successful transaction. By contrast, women in the same context do not show changes in their testosterone levels. This implies

---

[6] This paragraph draws mainly on Chapts. 8 and 9 of Bohnet (2018).

the gender differences in biological terms. To borrow Beauvoir's expression we saw earlier, one *is* born a woman.

If this claim stands, does it mean that Beauvoir was wrong after all? It is given that oxytocin and testosterone are respectively associated with "female" and "male" characteristics. Furthermore, these hormones are more prevalent in the bodies of their respective sexes than their counterparts. Yet, there are phenomena which defy explanations in terms of these facts.

One episode is this: a restaurant near the Nakanoshima koen park in Sapporo has a large center table that seats about 10 people. Its central location on the floor permits good views from other tables around it. On top of that, it is in the limelight literally, as a spotlight is installed right above it. This arrangement is somewhat like a combat sport venue, where the center table is the "ring" and other tables are the spectator gallery. The establishment offers a big-eat challenge, serving a 2-kg giant Hamburg steak, which is to be finished within 30 min. Failing this, an entrant is obliged to pay for the consumption (approximately 3,000 yen, according to my vague memory). On occasions where several challengers step forward at a time, they are invited to the center "ring" table. I was about 17 years old when I braved the challenge, with two friends of mine. The restaurant staff made a public announcement, "Ladies and gentlemen, now we have a giant burger challenge. Our contestants, please proceed to the center table." We stepped toward the table, gravitating the attention of the galleries.

On the ring, we were accompanied by a short-haired gentleman probably in his 40 s and a slim young woman, barely 20. These two seemed strangers to one another. Altogether, it was five of us: two friends of mine, the gentleman, the young woman, and myself. As I observed the two strangers talking, I gathered that the man was no stranger to this kind of event, while it was the first time for the woman. He said a few words of reassurance to make her feel at ease, looking full of self-confidence, and she anxiously responded in few words. There was a huge clock on the table. The voice through a microphone set the scene in motion. "On your mark, set, and let's go!" I started devouring my piece. As time elapses, the body will send the signal to the brain to recognize the fullness of the stomach, but there is a time lag between the actual amount eaten and the brain recognizing it. My strategy was to tuck in as much as possible before my brain caught up. A few minutes into the challenge, a friend next to me moaned that he got burnt in his mouth. The gentleman carried on eating at his pace, making a conversation with the woman. He was eating extraordinarily slowly. I heard him talking about his previous experiences of eating challenges. Apparently, it was a beef steak competition. The woman listened, with some verbal acknowledgment on occasions, and she kept eating. She was constant in this, not too fast or too slow. Her meat patty was becoming smaller little by little. When I conquered about a half of my serve, my brain seemed to have caught up. I started struggling, and the friend next to me, as well as the other one, looked the same. I whispered to them, "Oh no, I left my wallet at home." Without my contribution, the three of us could not pay up the charge if we failed. If one of us succeeded in eating one whole plate, we would all be spared. It was a lie, but only in order to boost their morale.[7] "You're kidding!" Their eyes were watered. Meanwhile, the gentleman stopped when he only reached one third of his portion. He said to the woman next to him, "It seems that today's not my day. I'm afraid I must call it a day," then he left the table. There was an air of dignity in the way he walked away. Sometime later, I also gave up, sweating profusely. I only got to two thirds. My friends did not make it either. It was only the young woman now staying in the game. She kept going alone on the "ring," not changing her pace in the slightest. And finally, she swallowed her last piece of meat.

The knowledge of behavioral economics can explain this embarrassing episode of my past. It was the unwarranted self-confidence and poor risk assessment that drove the men to the giant Hamburg steaks. However, previous findings of research in this area do not sufficiently explain the young woman's behavior and her success. The reason why she was drawn to the big-eat challenge will be explored in the next section.

There is another point that does not fit to the economic explanations and which I still wonder about to this day: the behavior of the middle-aged gentleman. What on earth was he there for?

Are Women Born Non-Competitive or Do They Become Non-Competitive?

> "He dropped out school at age 17 and enrolled in a college in Yanagawa city to become a speedboat racer. This was an institution to which only one in twenty-five could be admitted. He passed the exam on his second attempt. Speedboat racers must strictly control their body weight. In order to complete the one-year course and make a debut as a professional racer, they need to maintain their weight below the regulation threshold. He was a young and healthy individual who was undergoing natural physical growth. He could not maintain his weight, which was the reason he left the college after six months. Then, he overcame his disappointment and successfully sat in the examination for the alternative certificate for college eligibility, which allowed him to take a standard university entrance examination to Seinan Gakuin University. In the end, he became a university student without losing time, as he would be if he followed a standard path in the education system."

In my introductory seminar for first year students, I told the students to make pairs, introduce themselves and talk about their expectations for the future. The class had an odd number of students, so I paired up with the odd one, a male student. Let us call him "Y." I listened to him describe how he came to this university, which is the story in the previous paragraph. He was medium height, well-toned, and quite likable. A good talker, he made me want to know more about him. Before I knew it, time was up, and the class dismissed. I was impressed by his history for its extraordinary detour. Subsequently, Y enrolled in my tutorial class in years 3 and 4. He was the kind of person easy to relate to, and also very intelligent. He could easily follow my chain of

---

[7] I seem to have intuitively known the importance of economic strategies even before studying economics.

thoughts, and his answers to my questions often superseded my expectation. When I asked him about speedboat racing, of which I knew nothing, he filled me with various information, from race rules to racer training methods and a day's proceedings for professional racers. One day, I was with my students in an evening party. Until that day, I did not know of the existence of female racers. Neither did I know that there were mixed-sex races, where female racers partook and competed under the same conditions as their opposite sex racers. It was quite unimaginable for me, but I was told that, in the world of the sport, this was pretty much a day-to-day affair. I was drawn to Y's fascinating stories and inundated him with endless questions. The takeaway was that races took place at several circuits across Japan every day, and that they recorded and kept various kinds of information, culminating in a rich database.

It is known that, generally speaking, men are more competitive than women.[8] The question I have is this: is this gender difference in the competitive attitude attributed to innate characteristics of each gender or generated as a result of this personal trait being developed after birth? Opinions are divided on this topic among researchers. As I have mentioned earlier, it would be a biological fact if there were a definite gender difference in innate testosterone levels. It could otherwise be a result of social conditioning, as "one is not born, but rather becomes, a woman" in the words of Simone de Beauvoir. An "*in-situ* experiment" was conducted to investigate this point. While Japanese society is often described with the term "male chauvinism"—men take precedence in social contexts, and women are dominated—I have an impression that the male dominance is in some way prevalent in many parts of the world to a varying degree. There are, however, communities in which the reverse is true. In these communities, women take precedence in social contexts. Two societies on the opposite extremes of this trajectory serve as test grounds to examine whether the difference in competitiveness between males and females is biologically determined or socially constructed. This was the approach taken by a study, examining the Maasai people of East Africa as the world's most male dominant community, on the one hand, and the South Asian Khasi people living in the northeast of India as the most female dominant community, on the other.[9] The study involved a game of throwing balls into a basket. The rules are that, in each community, a group of local residents compete among themselves. Forming a pair, each one throws ten balls, and the number of balls that go in the basket is the score, according to which a reward will be given. Before starting the game, participants are asked to choose one of the following two conditions:

(1) the score is directly translated to the value of reward, or
(2) the score will be trebled before it is translated to reward on the condition that the game is won, but no reward will be paid out if lost.

Clearly, the latter condition gives a more competitive edge to the game. The outcome of the experiment showed that, among the Maasai people, men were more

---

[8] Bohnet (2018: chap. 8).
[9] Bohnet (2018: chap. 9); Gneezy and List (2014: chap. 2).

likely to choose the competitive condition for the reward payment, which is in line with the previous research. With the Khasi people, however, it was primarily women who selected the competitive option. These outcomes suggest that the gender difference in competitive attitude is a socially formed phenomenon. Nonetheless, this is not definitive as there may still be other variables at play ascribable to the differences between the cultures of East Africa and South Asia.

In the gender difference, very few field studies have been conducted in Japan, and I knew that, in this country, there was a professional sport in which women competed among men with equal opportunities and with some degree of success: Speedboat racing. I was joined by a leading figure of gender studies, Alison Booth, to conduct an experimental study using the unique setting of the Japanese speedboat racing world.[10] There are currently about 1,600 active racers. Of these, female racers account for about 20%. Six vessels enter a race at a time. While most of the competitions are single sex races, there are a few mixed-sex races. They are randomly assigned to single and mixed-sex races. In these, male and female compete under the same conditions. Winners will, for sure, earn winning prize money. There are some races taking place almost every day at some of the 24 race circuits in the country. There are 12 runs scheduled in a day. Data are collected from each racer, from the individual performance to the play results, amounting to an enormous database. Given this, we succeeded to collect more than 10,000 sets of data on the mixed-sex races. The data are longitudinal in the sense that information on particular racers covered a multiple number of competitions they ran, making it possible to follow their performance over time. This enabled us to analyze the results in terms of variables other than the racers' competence, especially to compare and identify differences in performance between mono-sex and unisex races.

One of unique characteristics of Japanese speedboat racing is the *flying start* system. Competitors are each assigned a pit number, but before a race starts, there is a 60-s maneuver time, during which they leave their respective pits and slowly move toward the start line, negotiating their ways to secure inner lanes at the start. This is very interesting to watch, as the running racers tactfully maneuver their boats toward more advantageous lanes while dodging their competitors. As the initial pits are predetermined, from 1 to 6, if no competitors dared to cut inside the ones in inner lanes, their starting lanes would be fixed as initially assigned. In other words, if the racers are not ambitious enough to play out the lane negotiation, the boat in pit No. 1 will take the innermost lane. The data include the pit numbers and starting lane numbers, which can be used to identify who negotiated their lanes successfully, indicating their competitive attitude. It is important to note, however, that there is a penalty for blocking the course of other boats by cutting in dangerously. This will result in disqualification and the racer will be denied entry to prestigious races (with high prize money) during the same season no matter how well he or she has been performing up to this point.[11] One mistake, and a top-ranking candidate for a

---

[10] Booth and Yamamura (2018).

[11] It is noted that some high-prize races set qualifying requirements based on racers performance in the same season.

champion of all 1,600 competitors can be dismissed from the racer-of-the-year league table. This means that racers need to have competitiveness, technical excellence, and rational judgment—they need to dare and secure inner lanes if they want to win the race, and they are under pressure not to commit foul negotiation of courses, otherwise their winning records so far will amount to nothing. Now, the analysis resulted in the following findings:

(1) male racers are more likely than female ones to win in a "unisex" race,
(2) female racers are less competitive in a unisex race than in a women's race during the flying-start lane negotiation, and
(3) no difference in the probability of committing a foul play between men and women. The probability of foul play for female racers is constant between unisex and women's races.

Overall, male racers are more competitive and successful without making foul maneuvers. Their counterparts are less competitive in unisex races and lose the chance of winning. The question is, are these differences attributed to innate nature or environmental conditioning formed through past experiences of racing?

Alison and I have been conducting additional analyses to investigate this point, for which we use the race performance records of all racers covering their entire career from the beginning and explore how their behavior in races changed over time. So far, we have found that both male and female racers show a tendency of being less competitive in the early days of their career, hence fewer wins. As they become more experienced, they grow more competitive and make more successful runs. There are no gender differences in this regard. An interesting observation is that female racers tend to be less competitive than the other sex members in the beginning, but they grow competitive more quickly as they gain experience, and this tendency is more prominent in the context of women's races. Their experience-based competitiveness, however, does not match up to that of men in unisex races.

A postulate scenario may help to understand and interpret these findings. It goes as follows: women are less competitive and more disinclined to compete than men by nature, but if they proceed to spend their adolescence years at girls' school, they have to face fierce competition among their peers and grow highly competitive, whereas in unisex schools, they will develop competitiveness after all, but not to the same extent as they would in girls' schools. Following this logic, we can make an account for the young woman who conquered the gigantic Hamburg steak. We assume that she learned what it meant to be competitive in the world of girls' school peer competitions. She then gained experience through women-only competitions such as big-eat parfaits or cakes. Convinced that she could win, she decided to take to the "ring," a unisex challenge of giant burger steaks. Behind her feminine front was, so one believes, her confidence for a victory backed by her track record.

Has Beauvoir's claim, "one is not born, but rather becomes, a woman," been refuted by the speedboat racing study? Apparently, "one is not born [a woman]" is not feasible because there is the biological aspect of female sex, that is determined beyond the influence of social construction. However, there is an element of truth in "becoming a woman." Being in a women-only environment, one becomes a strong woman, whereas in a gender-mixed environment, one becomes a feminine woman.

My former student Y graduated and got himself a job in an office, leading a busy life. I continue with my research in speedboat racing. This is a world of wonder, a treasure trove for my academic work. When I have questions concerning that realm of profession, I give him a call. He always gives me detailed answers, citing time that may be little in his busy lifestyle. He is as bright as ever, and his answers as clear and precise as those he gave me as a student. I sometimes recall how we met, in my Introductory Seminar in April 2012. If the class had had an even number of students, or if the odd one had been someone else, I would not have found speedboat racing as a research topic. I still remember, on the final day of the class, Y made a suggestion: "Let's take a picture with all of us." The chance meeting with a student evolved into my major work. "A stone by the roadside" turned out to be my gemstone.

Are Women Born to Dislike Math, or Do They Grow to Dislike It?

> "If you're not tough it's hard to survive in this world; and if you're not kind then you don't deserve to survive."

This is a famous quote from Raymond Chandler's novel. Detector Philip Marlowe is a masculine, strong, and genuinely gentle creature of his stories. Born in 1888, Chandler experienced poverty in the world under the Great Depression, which drove him to start writing. His masterpieces were produced in the 1930s up to the 1950s, which covers the period of the Second World War. He produced this strong and resilient male figure during these turbulent times. I suppose there was a demand for it in American society at the time. His work subsequently inspired many hardboiled fiction writers across the world.

The first half of the quoted line refers to a condition for living as a man. It is the second half that has more weight—"if you're not kind, then you don't deserve to survive." The real world is full of strong men who are insensitive and self-righteous; physical strength is their only virtue. This is scientifically verified, as we have already seen early in this chapter that men have higher levels of testosterone. In economics terms, men with gentle disposition are of a rarity, and therefore of higher value. To rephrase it, these are men with high testosterone levels and personal integrity not failing to make efforts to increase their oxytocin levels. Admittedly, this would be the ideal hard to attain. All the more reason why Chandler's man has the timeless appeal that grabs the hearts and minds of people.

Put into a different context, what would this famous line sound like? To help our imagination, I add these little three words.

> "*As a woman*, if you're not tough it's hard to survive in this world; and if you're not kind then you don't deserve to survive."

It gives out a significantly different connotation. Being strong, or "tough" in the first part of the line, does not seem to inspire the ideas of competitiveness or aggressiveness, but something different which has little to do with testosterone. It rather conjures up the kind of resilience and perseverance, like Oshin, that featured in Chap. 2, or a somewhat caricatured "post-war mother of resilience and determination." These are not personality traits that are innate to women, but more like the optional qualities that enhance the individuals, somewhat nonessential characteristics. Nonessential because, perhaps, there is a deep-rooted common normative notion of "a strong man protecting a vulnerable woman." The second half, that is "women do not deserve to survive if they are not kind," would sound like a confrontational challenge if these words are directed to the women of modern world. To those who have to juggle their full-time jobs and children to look after, these words could even be verbal violence. Japanese traditional social norm promotes the idea of women as "kind mothers devoted to their children," and if they fail to pay heed to this most basic norm and be kind, the line suggests, they do not deserve to survive. Meanwhile, they are expected to perform as well as men at work. This is an insurmountable dilemma in which working mothers find themselves.

Thus, the same phrase of words assumes considerably different meanings simply by changing the gender context. This happens because of the socially preconceived notion of gender identities, to which some specific gender roles are ascribed. Identity must have significant bearing on people's economic behavior. It is Rachel Kranton and Nobel Memorial Prize laureate George Akerlof who first introduced the notion of gender identity into economics.[12] They demonstrated the idea that gender-related norms cause men and women to behave differently even under the same physical conditions. A fundamental question arises at this point: do norms stay unchanged forever? It may well be possible that changes in economic conditions bring about changes in norms, just like people's values do, prompted by international trade, as we have seen in Chap. 2.

There is a common perception that men do well in mathematics and women do not. Having this as a norm would actually drive girls to fare less well than boys in math classes at school. Would it then be possible to break away from this preconception of girls not being good at math by giving different economic conditions? Imagine that having skills in mathematics would bring opportunities for better-paid jobs in modern society, where analyzing data is an essential task. If circumstances did not allow women to use their skills fully, these would not be accounted for in their salaries. And if girls knew that this was the case, learning math would be, for them, not worthwhile, damping their academic ambitions. As a result, the girls' educational performance in math would be poorer than boys. In order to verify if this scenario holds true, I conducted a statistical analysis using an international survey data on secondary school students from across the world, in particular, where it concerned their educational attainment in math.[13] The data was taken from the 2012 PISA academic performance assessment conducted by the OECD. This assessment surveys

---

[12] Akerlof and Kranton (2000).

[13] Yamamura (2019).

Fig. 4.2 Wages of women and girls' math scores

15-year-old students from across the world, who undergo tests in math and other academic disciplines. The PISA data shows that, in general, girls perform not as well in math as boys do. To this set of data, I also added wage disparity between men and women in 62 countries. This 2011 data was taken from the Global Gender Gap Report by the World Economic Forum.

Figure 4.2 illustrates the results. The perpendicular axis is the difference of math scores between boys and girls. Greater values indicate higher scores for girls. The horizontal axis shows the range of wages for women. The values closer to 1 are interpreted that the wage disparity is smaller. It is evident in the figure that women's wages and math scores of girls are correlated. It follows that, greater economic benefit from studying math gives girls more incentive to engage in learning, and their academic performance improves. Furthermore, the figures revealed that women's wage level in one country corresponded to the girls' school attendance, such as not being late for or absent from classes, in the same country. In other words, the economic advantage derived from school education boosts students' morale to go to school and learn. Data were also taken from developing countries, where it is not uncommon that parents choose to send their children to labor in order to help household finances. If the educational investment in female family members gains a recognition that it generates more economic value, those parents might change their views, let alone school-age girls. They would certainly choose to send their daughters to school instead of to work knowing that the girls will have a better chance for high-paid jobs and be able to help the family finance better in the future.

Norms inherent in society are not permanent. People's personal values and views undergo changes, partly influenced by economic situations. This will result in the common perception transformed in the course of time, leading to different ways of thinking and/or working. Altering systems or policies may not change social norms overnight. However, human sentiment is fluid, being altered by palpable changes in living standards. It may be as subtle a change as it is almost indiscernible, but it is taking place slowly but surely. When our grandchildren are fully grown up, in that remote future, I wonder, what would people in society make of that famous line of Raymond Chandler?

Equal Employment Opportunities for Men and Women, How Does It Affect the Difference in Height Between a Husband and a Wife?

In the early 1990s, Japan was in the height of a thriving economic bubble. One of the buzz words at that time was "men of WWT"—a term that expressed a man with desirable attributes for marriage, from the perspective of the women of the time: that is, a well-educated, well-paid, tall man. This "ideal" was later replaced by "MOM" when the economic bubble burst. It stood for moderate-earning, okay-looking, and mild-tempered. As economic depression lingered on, the image of ideal men for prospective husbands further evolved into "3Rs," that is, "respectful" toward women, "responsible" in household matters, willing to share chores and childcare, and "risk-free" in the employment department as a stable source of income. I am one of the "new generation" people of the post-modernization era, to whom the "men of WWT" sounds most relatable. This type of man was iconized in a top male fashion model, Hiroshi Abe. He had all the three attributes painted all over him. Subsequently, as the economy took a downturn, his popularity as a man of WWT dissipated, but alas, he reinvented himself as a seasoned actor with an impressionable character, alive and well today.

Back to the desirable husband materials, and let us take a look at the changes over time from an economic point of view. The transition of women's preference in men from the "WWT" to "3Rs" can be analogized as a change in women's demand structure in the marriage-seekers' market. To simplify the argument, we will limit our considerations to the desired attribute of body height. Previously, the mainstream trend in the marriage-seekers' market was a tall man, but this is not an absolute, but a relative, body height. To be precise, it is a man *taller* than the woman herself. Meanwhile, men preferred women who were shorter than them. Where their ideals were mutually satisfied resulted marriage. Therefore, a condition of a successful coupling for this market is that the man is taller than the woman. A change in women's preference in terms of their prospective spouses' heights modifies this condition, and as a result, the value of a difference in height between a husband and a wife diminishes. Writer Keisuke Hada, a 2015 Akutagawa Prize winner, said in an interview that he preferred a woman "taller than me." He was born in 1985, and thus grew up in the post-bubble era. It is not difficult to imagine that this kind of value orientation was uncommon among the men of WWT, but it may be shared widely among the men in the era of 3Rs. Moreover, the 3Rs as a set of desired attributes does not refer to the man's height. It seems to me that young people these days do not fuss about how tall or short their partners should be as much as older generations did.

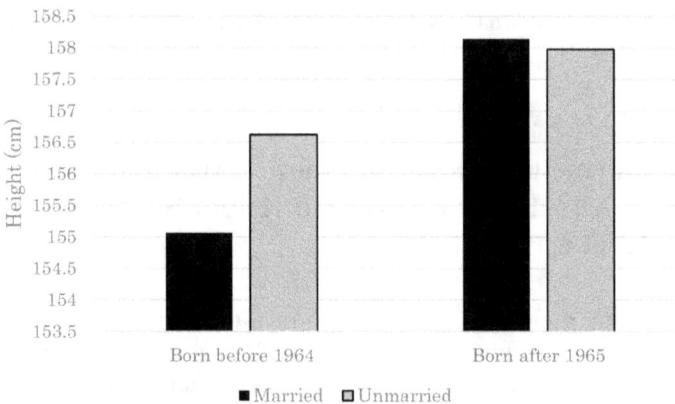

Fig. 4.3 Body height comparison between married and unmarried women

In Japan, the equal opportunity in employment act came into force in 1986. The act prohibited gender discrimination in workplaces and mandated that women were to be treated equally to men in terms of recruitment, employment, remuneration, and so on. A majority of the people who were finishing their higher education and seeking employment in this year would have been born in 1964. It is imaginable that these people experienced a degree of empowerment of women in the labor market, then this might have affected the perceived desirable attributes of women in the marriage-seekers' market. I addressed this point in a joint research project to investigate how the structural changes in the labor market affected people's values, especially about a person to marry.[14] There are physical differences between men and women, in which sense men are generally taller than women. It follows that more married couples would have the man taller than the woman even if the relative difference in height bore no significance to marriage seekers. In order to ascertain the relevance of this particular value shift, we need to run a cross-generational comparison of physical heights of married and unmarried population. In this research project, we used anonymized data of individuals, which included information about their birth year, gender, height, and marital status.

The main findings are illustrated in Figs. 4.3 and 4.4. Figures 4.3 shows average heights of sampled women by their marital statuses. The samples were reorganized into two subgroups, with the enactment of the equal opportunity act as a threshold, whether they experienced recruitment before this or after. Among the women who came into the labor market before the threshold, those married are shorter than their counterparts on average. This trend is reversed in the other group, that married women are slightly taller than unmarried ones. On the whole, it is recognized in these findings that, previously, short women were in greater demand in the marriage-seekers' market and more likely to get married, but later generations accorded less value to the body height of women.

---

[14] Yamamura and Tsutsui (2017a).

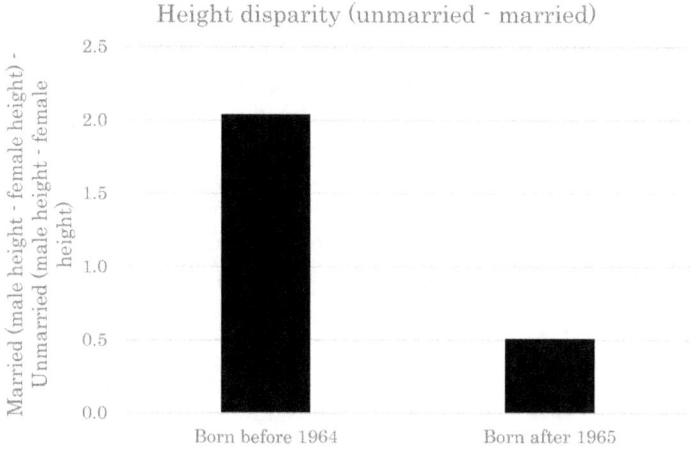

Fig. 4.4 Difference in male–female body height disparity between married and unmarried groups

Figure 4.4 shows the change in the value of relative body height by obtaining the difference between men and women in the subgroups. Although not shown in the figure, men's average heights were higher than those of women in all subgroups, that is, married/unmarried and before-/after-threshold. Thus, subtracting female height from its corresponding male height always yields a positive value. The left bar in Fig. 4.4 indicates the difference in average body height disparity among the people of the before-threshold subgroup, obtained by comparing married and unmarried subgroups. The value of 2 cm means that the gender disparity in average height for the subgroup of married people is greater than that of unmarried people by 2 cm, given that men are taller than women in both subgroups. This suggests that, within this older generation group, the greater the height disparity is between a man and a woman, the more likely that the two get married. This difference in height disparity diminished to 0.5 cm with the after-threshold group people. The significance of body height difference of a couple to their chance of marriage has thus shrunk to a quarter. Thus, this analysis reveals that the equal opportunity reform in the labor market devalued the body height difference between men and women in the marriage-seekers' market.

This tells us that the changes made to the labor market affected people's preferences in a person to marry, and it manifested in their choices of spouses and decisions to marry them. In other words, the act, which was introduced at the time when the men of WWT were sought after, changed the social dynamics and ultimately diminished the value of WWT assets. It follows that changing social structure, system, or rules appeals to human sentiments.

Hiroshi Abe used to feel uneasy about him being too tall, as rumor has it. He could not easily part with the public perception of him being a "good-looking man" when he started acting because his rather too tall physique limited the roles appropriate for him. In the post-bubble economy, women's perception of desirable men changed, and the value of tall men plummeted. The demand for this tall, good-looking actor thus diminished. He persevered with struggles and finally found a success in playing eccentric characters, establishing himself as a one-of-the-kind actor. His life story offers an important lesson to the Japanese economy. The country once enjoyed an extensive success founded on an economic structure that garnered a label, "Japan as Number One." The economic structure has been kept unchanged while the times have changed and it no longer serves the same purpose. This is analogous to the period in which being a tall man lost its value and the actor Abe struggled. What Japan needs today is a new economic structure that is relevant to, and competitive in, the modern world. Perhaps, to find a new, evolved Japan, we should look for some clues in the way Hiroshi Abe made his life a success.

Chapter 5
The Reason Why Working Husband and Housekeeping Wife Should Quarrel

I put on the radio at mealtime at home. One day, the letters-from-listeners part of the program was on a topic of farcical domestic situations. A letter described how the writer quarreled with her husband:

(Husband)   "Who do you think is putting food on the table?"
(Wife)   "I do, and I cook it for you, too!"

There is no clear-cut verdict on this call. The husband is implying that it is him who goes out to work and earns a living for his family, which is a reasonable claim. The wife asserts that she cooks for him, who is helpless in domestic matters without her, which may well be the case. This kind of miscommunication between a husband and a wife is not a laughing matter for economists. Disagreements similar to this do happen between economists and "non-economists." It reminds me of an olden-day hit song.

The Japanese folk singer, Masashi Sada, is a prolific musician, who writes and composes himself. One of his best-selling number is called *Kanpaku Sengen*, which translates as something like a declaration of authoritarian love. It became very popular as soon as it was released in 1979. The lyrics is a male voice narrative, which starts off being rather chauvinistic. In a gist, it goes like this:

> Before I take you as my wife, there are things you should know. As a woman, you do not assert yourself. You do what you are meant to do. I am a man, and I'll take care of the rest. So, do not argue and be with me.

Toward the end, the wording loses the male ego:

> I will be true to my love for you for as long as I live, so please stay with me.

I was a schoolboy when I heard this song, but I remember this just like it was yesterday. The song did not strike me as authoritarian for, I think, its balladic melody and the singer's gentle voice. Moreover, it must have been quite acceptable to those men who shared the Japanese male perspectives of the time. Looking at the lyrics today, it is clear that the monologue is making an utterly self-absorbed and incorrect claim. I wonder, four decades on, if people of modern society would positively support a song like this, which is so behind the times. Would you?

Today, a man so unwilling to discuss with, or understand, his female partner would possibly be fiercely criticized. Modern couples, I imagine, value highly of the efforts to understand each other through sincere communication. Let us consider if the attitude of the man in the song is justifiable from an economic perspective.

Income and household chores are both necessities in life. Where, in a couple, one does all the housekeeping and the other does work for income, this arrangement is called a division of labor. I will illustrate how a standard economist would understand it. Here is a question:

> Does it make sense if a professional cook in Chinese cuisine also cooks at home for his family?

You might say, "yes, the family may enjoy authentic Chinese dishes. Why not?" thinking the cook must be better at cooking than his wife. However, this answer does not warrant you a pass mark in a mid-term exam of an introduction class to economics at university. Here is why: the wife is not a professional cook, thus not generating income by cooking, but she does the job well for the family. Meanwhile, the husband cooks in his restaurant and customers pay for his service, but cooking for his family does not increase his income. Therefore, the *correct* answer is, "to maximize the daily income, the division of labor is desirable: the husband should stick to his restaurant and the wife should take care of cooking at home."[1] For our imaginary economist, thus, it makes more sense if a professional cook uses his vocational skills to generate income rather than waste time on his non-paying family. According to this line of argument, it is suggested that the "declaration of authoritarian love" song is, economically speaking, making a reasonable claim.

However, this argumentation does not convince me. Human nature does not make room for such a simplistic analysis. It is problematic that the argument presupposes the affection for one's spouse to be only variable in terms of money or in relation to other individuals. The affection for one's spouse, however, must depend on the relationship between the two individuals. It is certain that the division of labor is an efficient way to increase income, but we must ask ourselves, are we not giving up something very important in exchange for it? This is the question I would raise in my "*ninjo* economics." Assuming that a married couple has a task that involves both of them, this would foster and nurture confidence and sympathy between them. We all need a partner to share a life with through good times and bad times. Think of women with small children. They are under considerable stresses, both physically and mentally, to handle so much on a daily basis. With the changes in conventional family arrangements, they no longer live near their parents, who might otherwise have been able to help. Given this situation, their husbands' participation in household chores would be all welcome. It would give their wives a great deal of satisfaction. Greater satisfaction of the wife would improve the family life for the husband. This, however, comes with a drawback: the longer he spends for sharing household duties,

---

[1] Readers may find more details in Nishimura (2006: 149–153).

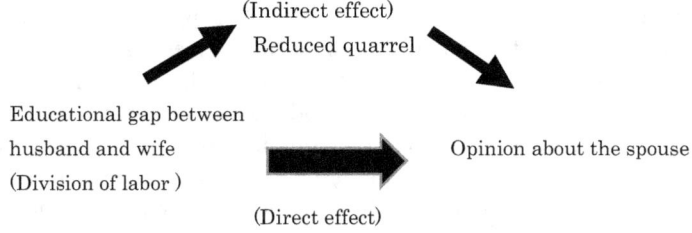

Fig. 5.1 The effect of division of labor on the marital relationship

the lower his income becomes. Thus, sharing domestic tasks between the couple is not all advantages.

One of my joint research projects looked into how the division of labor in marriage affects the frequency of quarrels and levels of satisfaction about the spouse.[2] To run a statistical analysis, I collected data from individuals who were due to marry someone in the near future. I asked them to evaluate their spouses and report the number of times they had an argument for the previous one month. I repeated the survey with the same individuals monthly for 37 months. The data thus collected covered the periods before and after their weddings, enabling us to see how their evaluations changed, the change, that is, over the threshold of relationship status between a girlfriend (boyfriend) to a wife (husband). The data also include the educational history of the participants and their partners. Here is the assumption for the analysis: whether a couple adopts the division of labor in their marriage depends on the levels of income, that are proportionate to educational qualifications. In general, people with higher levels of education have more chance for finding a better-paid job. A great gap in educational levels between a husband and a wife, for example where one is a university graduate and the other only had secondary school education, may well result in the former having a job and the latter occupying himself or herself with domestic chores. This was the case with my parents—my father had university education, and my mother did not have educational opportunities after secondary school. In their case, he went out to earn a living, and she stayed home doing her housewife things, just as the standard economics theory prescribes. With couples whose education levels are more or less equal, they are more likely to choose that both of them have a job. Based on these assumptions, we have a hypothesis that the division of labor is prevalent among couples with a wide disparity in final qualification levels.

The analytical framework is as follows: it is assumed that the division of labor causes to lower the opinion about the spouse, for not having the same levels of confidence or sympathy that would be generated by engaging in common tasks. Take this as a direct effect of division of labor in marriage, illustrated by the bottom arrow in the Fig. 5.1. Meanwhile, the division of labor reduces the time the couple spends together or discuss domestic issues. If they shared housekeeping tasks, it

---

[2] Yamamura and Tsutsui (2017b).

would raise the chance of bickering or disagreements happening. Fights in marriage affect their relationship: discontentment about the partner may lower the opinion about him or her. Therefore, dividing responsibilities of husband and wife, between income-generating work and housekeeping work, reduces the chance of quarrels, and therefore prevents the adverse effects on their opinions about the other, plus increases the household income. Take this as an indirect effect of division of labor, which is shown by the two upper arrows in the figure. Thus, the direct effect of division of labor is to lower the opinion about the spouse while the indirect effect raises it. Then, the overall effect can be measured by subtracting the negative direct effect from the positive indirect effect.

Calculation of the data yielded the following outcomes:

(1) couples that adopt the division of labor have fewer arguments after marriage,
(2) couples with fewer arguments after marriage have higher opinions of their spouses (indirect effect), and
(3) couples that adopt the division of labor after marriage have lower opinions of the spouses (direct effect).

These outcomes support the effect of division of labor on the marital relationship as illustrated in the Fig. 5.1. A comparison between the direct and indirect effects showed that:

(4) the direct effect is 10 times more powerful than the indirect effect! Therefore, the division of labor in marriage ultimately lowers the opinions about each other.

These findings conjure up a man's life like this: he comes home from work very late, absolutely worn out after a long day at work, his family has gone to bed, and he finds his dinner set on the table, which he reheats in the microwave; when the machine bleeps, he takes the plate out and returns to the table, to his usual seat, and starts eating by himself, feeling unfulfilled; his wife is a housewife; in the first year of their marriage, she used to wait for her husband and share the late dinner, discussing their respective days; he cannot remember when that changed, or any particular quarrel which resulted in him eating alone; he turns the TV on to fill the silence and realizes that he has not had a proper conversation with his wife for a long time; he senses that something is missing between him and his wife, but has never said anything about it to her, he feels that he has not the time or the courage to do so; he thinks to himself, "all these years, I have worked very hard to feed the family, and we have a comfortable life now. What went wrong to end up like this? Am I just a money-making machine to my wife?"

I wonder if men among the readers find that this scenario has a resonance to their actual lives. I would love to offer a female version of it, but alas, I am not blessed with the imagination and flair in writing to pull it off. If only I had the talent and produced the counterpart description, it would make the study more persuasive.

Still, the results of the analysis suggest that couples enjoy higher income and more material prosperity by adopting the division of labor, but it does not bring happiness. This is perhaps because this style of marital relationship forces the couple to sacrifice "little happiness," that cannot be compensated by financial sustenance provided by giving up the time to spend with their spouses. This being said, it does not simply follow that having a wife stay home necessarily leads to an unhappy life. My research suggested that couples with well-educated wives had higher income levels as the wives play a supportive role to their husbands, maintaining their physical and mental health and giving them advice and encouragement.[3] In this case, these women are not simply housewives, but they are part of their husbands' role as bread-winners in the household. Given this variance among the married couples with working husbands and housekeeping wives, this arrangement itself is not a significant determinant of their happiness; rather, it is the effort to share their lives in a matrimonial union based on good mutual communication. The secret therefore is the efforts to build and maintain a relationship that thrives in good times and endures bad times.

Before closing this section, I should put the readers' minds at ease. Here is my answer to the "Chinese kitchen cook" question:

> well, if the husband shared the cooking chores at home, it might increase the chance of having arguments with his wife, but "adversity strengthens the foundations," as the proverb goes. It may dampen the efficiency (income), but it is important to share the little moments in life. The mutual love, which goes beyond material consumption, will bring you and your spouse happiness. "Man shall not live by bread alone," as they say.

Why Do People Seek Marriage?

A novel entitled *A Perfect Marriage* was published in UK in Spring 2018. The author is an Australian best-selling writer, Alison Booth. She has a full-time job, and the creative work is mainly her weekend occupation. In an interview, she described that this arrangement suited her because her children were already independent and her husband often worked on weekends, and also writing allowed her to leave her day-to-day reality behind for a while.

It was May 2018 that I wrote to my research partner Alison about the joint project on the labor market in Japanese speedboat racing, telling her that I found something new and suggesting that we should continue this project. Her response was positive, only that she could not make time before October as she had just published her new novel a week before she received my email, and she had many engagements to attend to in relation to the launch. The readers must have guessed by now that the author of *A Perfect Marriage* is the Alison my research partner. She studied for a Ph.D. in the United Kingdom and stayed in the country for more than 20 years, during which period she taught at the University of Essex as Professor of Economics and also assumed the position of President of the European Association of Labour Economists and editor-in-chief of the association's journal, *Labour Economics*. Today, she is back in her own country, Emeritus Professor at the Australian National University.[4]

---

[3] Yamamura and Mano (2012).

[4] In my workplace, that is Seinan Gakuin University, I address academic colleagues professors if they are specialists in non-economics disciplines as it is customary to do so in their circles.

There are a few economists who produce literary work. For example, there is Kenneth G. Elzinga, who writes detective novels with his insightful expertise in economics well integrated in his stories. Many such economists part-time fiction writers leverage their knowledge in economics in their writing. Given that Alison is a prominent figure in the areas of female in labor power and economics of the household, her latest novel *A Perfect Marriage* does seem to be closely relevant to her field of specialization. However, her stories are written in a beautiful, lyrical language, without a hint of academic economics. Her previous work includes a novel set in a fictional Australian city, where a story unfolds in the past, and one that revolves around the protagonist's memories from school days. In both cases, the temporal axis is an important element. She does all the necessary homework to give her stories an authentic edge, visiting key places in the real world and gathering information from newspaper archives, documents, etc. She uses her real name as the author, but I imagine that many of her readers may not realize that Alison Booth is also a well-known economist.

The economist Alison is an active researcher, publishing many peer-reviewed papers in academic journals. When I worked with her for the first time on a joint research project,[5] I noticed, in the first draft, that she included Tim Hatton in her acknowledgment, thanking for his insights on the research subject. I wondered who he was and why his name was mentioned, for the paper had not been presented at any conference or study group. I looked him up and found that he was an expert in econometric history. I was puzzled why on earth an economic historian was interested in an empirical study about the Japanese speedboat racing world. I wrote to Alison, asking about this, and it turned out that Tim Hatton was her husband. It is not uncommon that two economists married to one another have some work published jointly, but Alison and Tim did not have any joint paper or co-authored publication under their names. I went through Alison's past papers and saw that Tim was mentioned in the acknowledgments of many of them. Alison Booth is such a person whose perspectives on female labor issues and economics of the household are enriched as she moves between her work and family, as well as between economics and novels.

Now, let us turn to the subject of marriage and consider it in economics terms. First, we delve into the psyche of individuals who get married.

Meanwhile, we academics in economics tend to address someone senior as professors, otherwise in a more familiar manner, with the title, such as mister and ms. I personally use "professor" if I have ever been taught by the individual in question, and use the standard suffix to everyone else. This culture of economists' academia is pretty peculiar by Japanese standards. Only the exception for me is to address as professor if I know this person prefers it.

With economists outside Japan, it is even more relaxed. You use "professor" when you address someone for the first time, then see how it goes from there. More often than not, you move on to given names with each other soon after that. To carry out a joint research project, you definitely need to be on first-name terms with your counterparts. Unless that person is extraordinarily eccentric, this is the case no matter how prominent he or she may be. So, my calling Professor Booth by her first name would translate in the context of Japanese academia as addressing her by her surname with a standard suffix for "Ms" (*Booth-san*) or with a respectful one for a teacher (*Booth-sensei*).

Subtleties of humanity are at play even in the world of academic researchers.

[5] Booth and Yamamura (2018).

We put the following question to those who are about to be married:

Why are you getting married?

Possible answers include:
A-1: because I love the person I am marrying,
else,
A-2: because my parents (or others) take the trouble of matchmaking, and
A-3: because my friends are also married.
Otherwise, these may be also possible:
A-4: because the bride (or groom) is very wealthy, or
A-5: because the bride (or groom) has a well-paid job.

Answers 4 and 5, obviously, imply that marriage is considered based on economic thinking. It is the aspiration to attain materially enriched lifestyles for the financial wealth that comes with the person to marry. In economics, Answer 1 is construed as consuming the marrying partner, Answer 2 is explained as a form of coercion, particularly if this person is somewhat dependent on his/her parents (or obliged to the matchmaker), and Answer 3 is taken as a case of so-called "peer effects," which describes the influences of members of a community to dictate a person's decision-making. Fashion trends are one of the examples that are explained by this notion.

Not all married couples in the world are successful in maintaining lasting, good relationships in their marriages, like Alison and Tim, so we put another question to those who are about to get divorced:

Why are you getting divorced?

To draw a parallel to the answers about getting married, possible answers would be:

A-1': because I no longer love my partner,
A-2': because my parents (or others) advise me to leave the partner,
A-3': because my friends are also getting divorced,
A-4': because my partner's assets have significantly diminished, and
A-5: because my partner earns far less than before.

Reasons for deciding to get a divorce are more complicated than those for deciding to be married. Economics presupposes that individuals make decisions with long-term implications considered. Analyses are therefore based on this notion of rational agent. This taken on board, people would not go through a marriage if they knew they would eventually get divorced. Otherwise, they would be tying the knot with a future divorce written in. Well, that already sounds like a trouble in the making, like a plot for a detective novel. However, it is hard to believe that many people scheme a strategic marriage with a clear intention of divorce to follow. I wonder whether my readers would agree.

All in all, I assume that most people who come to break up their marriages never expected it to happen when they got married. I imagine their inner thoughts to be something in the line of:

What was I thinking to marry someone like this? I'm such an idiot!

with a hint of regret. Then, does this mean that these people lack the kind of rationality that economists attribute to their postulate "people"? No, that is not true. Rational people, too, do get divorced. Then, why?

Standard economists assume that people do not change their preferences. If someone who loves ramen one day changes their mind and eats it no more, it could be because this person has become richer and can afford more expensive, fancy food, and ramen no longer appetizes them, which does not count as a change in preference. In this case, the person simply chooses to eat something else due to the change in financial circumstances. Alternatively, suppose that the person simply had too much of it. In this case, too, economists do not consider this a change of preference because economics presupposes that consumption in excess will lower the satisfaction the commodity offers. Applying this approach to a partner in marriage, falling out of love is not a change in preference, but changes in circumstances. Thus, Answers' 4 and 5 do fall squarely in this economic framework. Rather, this explanatory model is necessary. As for Answers' 2 and 3, the decision to divorce may be understood to be made under the influence of other people.

Even so, standard economics does not cover all possibilities. It must leave out some reasons for a change of heart that results in a breakup that cannot be ascribed either to changes in circumstances or external influences. So, we will take a deeper look into this topic through the vision of economics with a touch of humanity.

What Comes to the Minds of Smokers at the Sight of Their Children?

I wrote about the film *Bohemian Rhapsody* in Chap. 1, that it attained a phenomenal success. Normally, most commodities gradually lose their attraction as more is consumed, and films are no exception. This is one of the principles the introductory textbooks of economics teach in early stages. In the case of films, new releases can be enjoyed, perhaps online, without paying a lot of money by giving them a bit of time. Even if you wanted to watch a particular film as soon as it comes to cinema, watching it once would be enough. It is not worth watching it twice. You would perhaps spend that money and time to see other films that interest you, or to do something else that you enjoy doing.

If you knew the plot in advance, you might lose the incentive to make your way to the cinema. For this reason, film trailers take the form of teaser ads, keeping the best part a secret. Film reviews online, also, take a cautious approach not to disclose the whole story to people who have not watched the film, and give people the "spoiler" warning if the texts describe the crucial part or climax. These things considered, it is the stories that people consume, rather than the films. *Bohemian Rhapsody* is not at all like other films. Not a few people watched it more than once—twice or even five or six times. A TV program reporting on a bar frequented by Queen fans featured a multiple number of individuals who claimed to have seen it more than 10 times. Someone who said he saw it "three times" appeared somehow apologetic in the same TV show. This phenomenon clearly defies the textbook explanation.

In fact, this Queen movie is not unique in this respect. And there is an economics argument that seeks to explain these special cases: a theory that accounts for the consumption of goods that induce addiction, like cigarettes. This economic theory defines these "addictive commodities" as items that stimulate more desire for them as they are consumed.[6] Once addicted, it is difficult to shake off the habit, which many of the readers would have witnessed in the behavior of smokers around them. Whether addiction is good or bad—economists are divided on this question. I have treated films in my past study, in which I revealed that they are indeed an addictive commodity.[7] I must confess that I have been mildly addicted to *Bohemian Rhapsody*. I felt so emotional watching it in cinema, and I enjoyed the fulfilling sensation, which in itself is not a bad thing. Smoking is different. I am not a smoker myself. I would advise my smoking students to quit the habit. Why? There are two reasons.

(1) Smoking is harmful to human health, and it is scientifically proven that smoking shortens the life expectancy, and
(2) secondhand smoke that enters the environment and is inhaled by people is about three times more harmful than the smoke which the smoker inhales through a filter.

Reason (1) is contended: some economists consider it to be a matter of the smoker's own judgment, but others still take issue with such an opinion. I am the latter because the problem is not confined within the smokers themselves. Chances of diseases afflicting smokers of many years significantly increase in their 60s and thereafter. They will push up national medical expenses, and increasing social security cost leads to a strain on government budget. From a long-term perspective, the burden is passed on to our children's generations.

As for Reason (2), I have never met anyone who blatantly disagrees with it.

From the above, one could argue that the blame is not attributed to what economics defines as addictive commodity, but to the harm smoking causes to others and to the environment.[8] Compared to this, the Queen movie has the characteristics that are opposite to those of smoking.[9] You watch it and come out emotionally exalted, then you tell a friend how wonderful it was and invite them to the cinema. You go to see it again, this time with your friend. The joy derived from the film is amplified by sharing the experience. It is not simply one plus one makes two. Watching *Bohemian Rhapsody* with someone boosts the "Queen euphoria" far more than watching it alone. According to my previous study, people with many personal connections

---

[6] Becker and Murphy (1988).

[7] Yamamura (2009b).

[8] This type of harm is called "negative externality" in economics. Solving it is one of the major themes in economics.

[9] This is called "positive externality" in economics.

are more likely to enjoy watching films in cinema.[10] Films themselves have the element of sharing the enjoyment. The effect is short-lived, and this is why the demand pattern can be explained by the standard principle of economics. However, *Bohemian Rhapsody* produces a long-lasting, powerful effect of watching it with someone else, which results in prompting people to want to enjoy the film in cinema, sharing the experience with many fellow viewers. The last scene reveals the reason for this: Queen's appearance on the Live Aid stage. It is because the band's songs are essentially a form of entertainment that invite people to join in, generates a sense of inclusive bonding, and distributes the sense of happiness among the participants.

The above is the answer to the opening question of this section. Now we turn to the cigarette consumption behavior. I once analyzed the relationship between smoking and another major addictive commodity, that is, alcohol.[11] In olden days, it was not uncommon to see people enjoy drinks in bars with cigarettes in their hands. Only certain types of drink houses remain to be a haven for these people nowadays as the non-smoking policies pervade across public and communal spaces. There are very few places left for them to be able to enjoy their smokes to their hearts' content. Alcohol and cigarettes are, in some sense, like morning cereal and milk—you cannot have one without the other. In this sense, we can say that they fall in the same category.[12] However, there is a significant difference between these addictive commodities. Drinking alcohol in itself is harmless and does not cause a nuisance if consumed moderately. Alcohol consumption coupled with smoking, however, is an unwelcome behavior after all. The idea that came to my mind was a separation of these two preoccupations. I hypothesized this idea: in residential areas with closely bonded communities, people are less likely to smoke when they have drinks because they feel obliged to spare others the unpleasantness of the secondhand smoke. I collected and analyzed data, the result of which supported the hypothesis. This suggests that personal relationships in community are a clue for reducing the consumption of addictive commodities.

Relationships in community are variable depending on the nature and social or emotional proximity. Obviously, individuals who are exposed to the smoke-related risks and unpleasantness the most would be the family members of smokers. Based on this idea, I planned to investigate, with a joint research partner, how smokers would change their smoking behavior on account of their family members who share the same households, using individual-level data.[13] We used a cohort of pre-marital individuals and conducted a monthly survey for three years, totaling 37 sessions. With some arrangements to questions, the data gathered through the survey enabled us to follow up circumstances of these individuals from when they were in a pre-marital relationship, in marriage, during a wife's (for women, their own) pregnancy, and after childbirth. The data also included information about their drinking/smoking behavior at each time of survey session. The analysis revealed the following:

---

[10] Yamamura (2008).

[11] Yamamura (2011c).

[12] This is called "complementary" in economics.

[13] Yamamura and Tsutsui (2019b).

(1) both men and women reduced their alcohol and cigarette consumption during pregnancy and after childbirth.

This outcome illustrates an overall tendency on average, but it does not reveal whether the decline of consumption was attributed to a number of individuals completely giving up or it was simply because the majority of people reduced their consumption. To find out, we ran a further in-depth analysis and came up with the following results:

(2) women stop drinking alcohol when they become pregnant or give birth while men stop short of giving up drinking, and
(3) marriage, pregnancy, and childbirth increased the chance that women ceased smoking completely; for men, marriage and childbirth did increase the probability of them giving it up.[14]

These findings tell us that men and women alike modify their behaviors when they have their spouses and children around, in order to prevent undesirable effects of their consumption. More interestingly, women stay away from alcohol after childbirth. Although consuming alcohol does not physically affect people who are nearby, it does a fetus inside a pregnant woman if she drinks. Women generally spend longer time caring for their babies, and they tend to shun alcoholic beverages to avoid the risk of mistreating their children under the influence of intoxication, which may happen to cause a fatal incident. Meanwhile, men reduce the amount they drink, but because the effects of their drinking on their family members are perceived to be small, they do not give up drinking. By contrast, the adverse effects of smoking are far greater, and both sexes are compelled to give up smoking.

I was watching TV, and on the screen I saw a mother and daughter being interviewed outside a cinema, just after they watched *Bohemian Rhapsody* together. The mother says she is a decade-long fan of Queen, and she loved the film so much that she has come back again with her daughter. The daughter says she enjoyed it very much and was happy to share it with her mother, who is looking very contented, standing next to her. It is obvious that the "Queen film" has the power to strengthen the family bond, and this is because it shows "the truth that humanity longs for." Next time, I would take my rebellious daughters with me to see the film again for my third time. I hope they will feel this "something special," too.

Having a Working Mother, Does It Determine a Man's Choice of a Woman He Marries?

In 1992, the buzzwords of the year people nominated in the post-bubble-economy Japan included "Fuyuhiko-san," which was subsequently awarded grand prix.

---

[14] While pregnancy was associated with reduced numbers of cigarettes men smoked, it was not clear if it made them decide to quit smoking. Presumably, the difference from the case of women is the indirect nature of the effect of smoking to the unborn baby in the mother's body.

Fuyuhiko-san is the name of a lead-role character of a TV drama series, *Zutto Anata ga Suki Datta*, who was portrayed as the ultimate "omther's boy". The series was a great success, with record-high viewing rates, and the actor Shiro Sano, who played Fuyuhiko, became a top star. Being a fictitious figure, this man cannot be taken as a generalizable representation of what a "mother's boy" actually is but he caught the nation's imagination and stirred a sensation among the viewing public, which suggests that people could easily identify someone they knew who mildly resembled this nerdy character. There are economic studies that explored the prevalence of men with this disposition in society.[15] However, the implications of being a "mother's boy" are not like how it was caricatured in the TV series. We need to pay attention to mothers' notable attributes. It is both possible that these attributes have a positive or undesirable impact on their children. We have examined in Chap. 4 how equal employment opportunities between men and women had an effect on the preferences of personal attributes sought for in marrying partners. This time, we will look at working mothers and whether their laborer status has a bearing on their sons' choice of types of women for a marriage.

Raquel Fernández, the economist I referred to in Chap. 4, whom I met in an academic conference in Paris, conducted a joint study on American citizens and found that men raised by working mothers grow up to be married to women who are also active in the labor market.[16] These men grow up to form an ideology that embraces the idea of women having jobs, and also they meet and choose women who work, like their mothers. A similar analysis on Japanese men found out the following[17]: men raised by working mothers come to disagree with the idea of division of labor in marriage, which connotes that men go out to work and women stay home. Furthermore, these men disagree with the idea that working mothers are bad influence on the children's development. According to the research I conducted, in Japan, newly-wed men are more active in domestic work sharing if they grew up with working mothers, and the hours of domestic participation increases proportionate to the duration of their marriages.[18] In other words, working women as mothers have a bearing on their children's, and especially boys' formation of the values about female labor force participation, and influence their behavior in their adulthood.

As we have already seen, the division of labor in marriage lowers the couple's satisfaction levels about their relationship. Moreover, working mothers stimulate their children to develop the values that are congruent with the new era.[19] The interactive relationship between the opposite sexes thus lead to a minimization of

---

[15] Fernandez et al. (2004), Kawaguchi and Miyazaki (2009). It is my own interpretation of these studies to be focused on the "mother's boy" phenomenon. They are more generally understood to support the claim that female influence on sons leads to social changes.

[16] Fernandez et al. (2004). According to Google Scholar, a scholarly literature database, this paper has been cited 670 times in various academic studies (accessed February 24, 2019). For the entire work by Fernandez, it is cited 10,286 times.

[17] Kawaguchi and Miyazaki (2009).

[18] Yamamura and Tsutsui (2021).

[19] I have treated cross-gender influences in this book, namely, from mothers to sons, from female teachers to male students, and from daughters to fathers. Other than these, I have also found that

gender disparity in values. To my mind, it is important that men and women make efforts to develop a mutually compassionate relationship and to better understand one another. Some might say that women have traditionally been assuming the role of a housewife, but I think it is arguable where this idea of "tradition" came from. In agrarian communities, all family members had their roles in cultivation work. The "housewives" emerged, probably, through the transition from pre-modern to modern, industrialized society.

Men who are raised by working mothers are supportive of their wives' labor participation. If there are more men like these, it may possibly lead to a richer diversity in workplaces. The labor market may increase its fluidity by turning more men broad-minded and flexible in their thinking. Maternal influence on male offspring would be a viable means for transforming society into such a form that is desirable for the future world. If this is the case, then, the mama's boy phenomenon is not such a bad thing—the negativity that comes with the term may be turned around, or perhaps, someone will come up with a new, more fashionable name for it. I may not be the best person to do it, but anyone out there could be. The readers, any ideas?

Does an Arrival of a Daughter Change Her Father's World View?

Imagine: a strict man of conservative values becomes a father to a daughter and changes into a gentle individual with a supportive attitude toward women's rights; a self-claimed wild economist with manly charms turns into a man who embraces his girly side when a daughter is born, starting to enjoy shopping with her to choose her pretty dresses.[20] Do you think it is unlikely? Evidence from a recent study suggests that the presence of a daughter has a significant impact on the values and behavior of her father, based on data analyses.[21] Similarly, it has been discussed whether, for a man, having a daughter will cause him to develop a prosocial disposition, which is more associated with women. If it is the case that men assimilate their values to the kind of feminine values discussed in Chap. 4 due to having a daughter, we may think that "men are born men, but acquire woman-like prosocial attitudes by the arrival of a daughter." In the previous chapter, I also mentioned that women favored ESG investment (i.e., corporate initiatives in social investment), and that schoolboys who were taught by female classroom teachers grew up to be inclined toward it. This

---

men are more likely to be sympathetic toward social participation by women if their wives are interested in politics (Yamamura 2010).

[20] Zak (2012).

[21] See for example, Oswald and Powdthavee (2010), Washington (2008). Furthermore, participation in child rearing increases the extent to which a father is influenced by the presence of a daughter (Borrell-Porta et al. 2019).

leads to the next question: would grownup men change their views to have a pro-ESG attitude if they had daughters? There is an insightful study to this question.[22]

This study looked not at subjective values of ordinary people, but at major American corporations and followed their ESG investment performance over time. The data in this study, therefore, are quantified and objective. The ESG investment is assumed to fluctuate depending on the policies set forth by the business management. The authors particularly looked into the changes in the family composition of the business managers. Do they change their views as they go through life events such as marriage, childbirth, and having children? In particular, does the presence of daughters affect their values, and if so, does this lead to an increase of the amount of ESG investment? To answer these questions, the authors gathered information relating to the life events of target executive officers from every possible source, such as online articles, newspapers, journals, etc. and identified if and when they had daughters.

These family composition data were linked with the data on ESG investment data of respective companies to create a unique dataset. It is then used to analyze whether corporate executives' decisions about ESG investment of their companies had anything to do with their becoming fathers with daughters. Through an empirical analysis, they found the following:

(1) companies with executives who have daughters make ESG investment 9% more than the companies managed by daughter-less executives, and
(2) there are no differences in the ESG investment levels between companies with executives who have sons and their counterparts.

The investment size is significantly greater in companies with female executive officers than ones only with male management members. About 30% of the difference by the genders of the executives themselves equals to the increment of ESG investment by business managers with daughters. In other words, the birth of a daughter in a male executive officer's family reduces the gender gap in opinions about ESG investment by roughly 30%. Daughters, therefore, have an effect on their business executive fathers so that their investment decision-making has a more feminine touch.

We have thus established that the presence of a daughter becomes an influential part of her father's own being, and its power extends to his business decisions. It is true that I started working on the subjects presented in Chap. 4 and in this section after my daughter was born. According to my unofficial field research, fathers with both grownup sons and daughters do not change their countenances when talking about their sons, but about their daughters they soften up. The facial wrinkles clearly indicate that affection hormone (oxytocin) levels surge while thinking about their daughters. These "samples" are all eminent economists over 60 years of age. A Japanese professor of economics who is based in a prestigious American university was saying proudly that his daughter was a significant inspiration in his life.[23] Often,

---

[22] Cronqvist and Yu (2017).

[23] This professor confessed that he had an inspiration for a study while he was with his daughter in a circus tent, watching the show. The paper produced subsequently gave a crucial insight to an American economist, who then produced a piece of Nobel-prize-winning work.

economists are perceived to be callous and unfeeling creatures, but they definitely share the same characteristics as the man in the street. These findings as I have related in this section, that is, modern-day American executives' decision-making and the case about economists, serve as evidence of the universality of the world view that permeates the Ozu films.

What Changes Do Grandchildren Engender in Their Grandparents?

The story starts with an elderly couple from the small Hiroshima town of Onomichi, traveling to Tokyo to visit their grownup children. The children give them a somewhat lukewarm welcome, and Noriko (played by Setsuko Hara), wife of the son lost in the war, is the only one to treat them warmly. Feeling burdensome and uncomfortable, the parents cut their stay short and return home, but the old lady is taken ill soon after the long journey and passes away. The children come home at the news of their mother gravely ill, but they return to Tokyo as soon as the funeral is over. Finally alone, the father (played by Chishū Ryū) gazes at the calm of the inland sea off the shore of Onomichi. *The Tokyo Story* is a masterpiece of film director Yasujirō Ozu. In this film, he juxtaposes the deconstruction of family-centered communal life in regional towns and the rising urban culture that embraces individual-centric ideology and economic growth. Released in 1953, the film reflected the social context of the time in the background, that the rural population was migrating to urban cities at an accelerating rate. The industrial structure was fast evolving from the primary industry such as agriculture to the secondary and tertiary industries, and people flocked to large cities to find jobs. It was an inevitable development that young people left the web of their rural communities behind and pursued economic prosperity in cities. Consequently, family values started to decay. The film depicts various individuals responding differently to this development. The difference in attitude to the changing society is generational. Clearly, Ozu takes the old couple's perspective to view the deconstruction of family values in post-war Japan. This is reflected in photograph of the Family in Fig. 5.2. No judgment is made, only the sense of resignation to the social transition and reminiscence of the disappearing familial attachment linger.

Beyond the social metabolism is a future world, where the restraints of family and community connections are replaced by the modern sense of self, free choice, and autonomy. As it was mentioned in Chap. 3, the transition from community to market economy brought about material prosperity and dignity of an individual, which is a desirable change. The thriving economic growth of the time made it easy to believe in a better tomorrow and brighter future. The film acknowledges and affirms this, and yet there is a kind of indefinable sadness that permeates the story. The sense of resignation and sadness is glorified only in so far as there being a strong economic growth about to flourish. Economics teaches that something must be lost in order to gain something else. The reason *The Tokyo Story* remains to be an eternal masterpiece

Fig. 5.2 Photograph: A family in *The Tokyo Story*. © 1953 Shochiku Co., Ltd

is because it remembers the disappearing family values and rural life, being lost in exchange for the reality brought about by the fast-growing economy.

Turning our eyes to ourselves, what do we lose in the life of this transitional era, and what do we gain instead? Theories of economic growth provide a concept of steady state. This refers to a period following rapid growth, when growth rates decline, and eventually growth stagnates. It is analogous to us human beings in that we grow rapidly during the teen years, but the growth slows down in our twenties, and we stop growing further in our thirties. Thereafter, we start shrinking in our old age unless we try our best not to. Economic growth is just like our physical growth. All we can do as a mature society with its population fast aging is to stop or delay economic decay. Economic stimulus only has temporary effects. It never leads to a long-term transformation. It is important to acknowledge this fact. Turning a blind eye does not work, and eventually the reality will hit us. It would almost be like a world Kazuo Ishiguro, who we saw in Chap. 3, might treat in one of his novels. He has in-depth insights into the latest economic problems. And he is far more honest and sincerer than some economists are.

Does that mean, then, that Japan can only decline and perish as a society? No. Even though individuals get old, their children, and their children, live on, and as long as this chain of generations continues, society remains in existence. The society will be maintained as we trust the future to our descendants. I am no philosopher or sociologist. I will leave the abstract arguments aside, and instead, describe an empirical study on the subject of social continuity, which I currently pursue. One of the fundamental issues of concern across generations is the fiscal problems. As I argued in Chap. 3, the present fiscal problems will only cause a tremendous burden to our future generations unless funding is secured by raising the consumption tax rate. It is like our children will be made responsible for the debts their parents, that is us, have created. The burden would be obvious in a direct relationship such as one between parents and children, but when it comes to generational relation, it is difficult to perceive the problem because the government mediates the parties in this abstract relationship. While the make-shift economic policies are not permanent solutions, we are all aware of this. Rational individuals might think, knowing this, that they would be alright as long as the economy was sustained during their lifetime. Would they not think differently if they had their own grandchildren, who would be the ones to carry the burden? I think it is only humanly natural to wish for the success and happiness of their own flesh and blood. Take this as a premise, and if it is valid, it must follow that people who have grandchildren are more likely to agree with the consumption tax hike than their peers with no grandchildren. I personally gathered data and ran a statistical analysis. The tentative results supported my hypothesis.

There was another interesting finding: it is normal, even an intrinsic part of human sentiments, for anyone to seek profit while avoiding payment, or delay the payment as long as possible so that they can live comfortably for a longer period of time, on which note it seems a good idea to defer the payment of tax into future times so that it will be paid by someone else. It follows that older people would be against raising tax rates. However, my statistical analysis yielded a result contrary to this. It showed that older people are more supportive of the increase of tax rates. This might suggest that these people, approaching the stage of life where death becomes a relevant subject matter, begin to consider the meaning of life or care for the future of their nation. It could be that people become more aware of the temporal axis that connect their beings and the society that has nurtured them—the trajectory between the debt of gratitude and repayment of this debt.

The founding father of economics Adam Smith and the founder of neoclassical economics Alfred Marshall both started in moral philosophy and extended their perspectives into economics. Thus, those philosophical questions that one might be confronted with during one's adolescence, lie underneath the disciple of economics: what is life? how should one live? what makes one's life more meaningful? What stands at the frontier of modern economics is a broad sense of, and long-lasting, *giri ninjo*, which adolescence is oblivious to.

Chapter 6
What Came Out of the Spread of COVID-19?

Effects of School Closure on Parents' Working Styles

"A novel coronavirus disease is said to be spreading in other countries." This onlooker-mentality had suddenly to change on February 27, when the Japanese government announced a call for temporary closure of schools. Since then, our everyday life has undergone a palpable change, and three months have passed.[1] There are media reports on a daily basis about the numbers of new confirmed cases and deaths, as well as other economic indexes in relation to the COVID-19 pandemic. Data evidently show that there has been a significant impact on society.

What is then happening to us in a more immediate environment? Some foreign media report that there has been a sharp increase in domestic child abuse cases since the coronavirus pandemic has ensued. People are confined in their homes under lockdown measures, and this may be causing excessive stress, which some people may be taking out on their children. Elsewhere, a new term "corona divorce" has been in circulation. Couples who normally spend quite a lot of time away from their partners have so far maintained their relationships because of it, but now that they have no choice but to spend much longer in each other's presence, perhaps, they are reaching the end of their tethers. I am working on a joint research at present, with Professor Yoshiro Tsutsui of Kyoto Bunkyo University and others, on the impact of COVID-19 on people's domestic lives.

We administer an online questionnaire to approximately 3,500 individuals throughout Japan. Started in mid-March, the survey is repeated fortnightly with the same individuals. This follow-up style survey allows us to look into and closely analyze the changes in people's behavior and mentality in relation to the spread of the disease, related policies, and so on over time. In this chapter, I will describe what we have discovered so far from this study.

---

[1] The manuscript has been left unchanged in order to reflect the current situations at the time of writing.

The first survey was conducted about 10 days after the nationwide school closure had already begun. Children were spending time in their homes when they would normally be at school. For parents, they cannot leave their children alone at home, especially those in primary education, concerned about their educational and social well-being. Some studies in the economics of education and family suggest that appropriate presence of adults for an adequate amount of time has a significant implication to the development of children. Mothers who have no jobs may have been able to adjust their routines to the ad hoc situation caused by the school closure without much difficulty, but the question is working mothers—how did they respond? To probe the data in relation to this question, we extracted the data of individuals who had full-time jobs in offices and analyzed how their ways of working have been affected by the presence of school-age children.

The survey included questions about the respondents' situations concerning "work from home," as well as demographic information such as their gender, whether they have any children at elementary school or secondary school, and if they had their parents living in the same household. We ran a statistical analysis on these data and found the following:

(1) of the women in full-time employment, 42% of those who had children in primary education completely switched to working from home, and 26% did the same among those without children in primary education.

This result indicates that working mothers choose to work from home because they need to look after their young children, which is more or less a predicted outcome. We also found that

(2) of the men in full-time employment, only 3% of those who had children in primary education completely switched to working from home, but the figure for those without children in primary education was 21%.

The gender disparity among those without school-age children is a mere 5%, which may suggest that the equal participation in society is bearing fruit to some extent. However, the discrepancy within the male group is more than 15% attributed to the presence of children in primary education, a staggering three-fold difference compared to the gender disparity. In a sense, this is an unexpected result. One would imagine that, given the progress in creating a society that empowers women and the perceived increasing number of men willing to take part in childcare, men would also choose to work from home for their children, like women do. However, the data suggest the contrary. What is the explanation?

In the case of a double-income household, it suffices that one of the partners stays home to look after their children. The other can be out for work, which in itself does not raise a problem. The data shows that the wife chooses to work from home, and the husband leaves the domestic responsibilities, including their children, with her and goes out to his office. He could prefer working in the office to get out of the house, as it is suffocating to be confined in the home environment all the time. It seems unlikely that employers have authority over their choices because more men do choose to work from home if they do not have children to look after.

More interestingly, the presence of school-age children becomes irrelevant to couples as to their choices of remote working if their parent or parents lived with them. Working mothers can count on their parents to keep an eye on their children, so they have a choice (for the assumption that those elderly parents are able to give support in childcare, the data for this analysis precludes the cases where parents who share the same household are over 80 years old). Existing studies show that, in Japan and other countries alike, female participation in the labor force is encouraged if the grandparents' generation can take part in childcare. This is in alignment with our findings.

As for children in secondary education, their presence does not factor in the choice of remote working regardless of the gender of these full-time workers. It can be explained that the need for working from home diminishes as their teen-age children can manage themselves autonomously to an extent. In classic economics terms, our findings are a result of people's rational actions and ones that make economic sense. One partner who is better able to take care of children looks after them while the other who is more capable of earning income invests time and effort in productive activities. Where the children are sufficiently mature, they both choose to work to increase the income instead of using the time for childcare, the result of which is a greater household income. Only that, according to a recent elaborate empirical study, teenagers deprived of sufficient parental guidance are more likely to develop trouble-making, anti-social behaviors. Assuming this being the case, those parents may be spoiling the future of their teenage sons and daughters by opting for immediate gain on their household incomes.

In any case, the study has revealed that gender disparity in the choice of work styles does exist in twenty-first-century Japanese society. According to the 2020 Global Gender Gap Report, Japan ranks in the 121st of 153 countries in terms of the gender parity in society. Given this, our findings are nothing unexpected. While economic studies overseas make a headway into the effects of the COVID-19 pandemic— some suggesting that white-collar female workers are more likely than their gender counterparts to be in a position that does not choose where to work, hence more at ease with working remotely—a positive interpretation that the post-COVID world may offer more opportunities to women may be just a partial view of the real state of affairs.

As far as our findings go, they present a picture that, in white-collar double-income households, the wife handles her work as well as housekeeping and children while the husband focuses on his work. It is possible that the work-load imbalance between husband and wife will be exacerbated in the post-COVID world. Wives' discontentment, frustration, and stress may be amplified and, eventually, come to a point of explosion. They need to let off steam, but who can they talk to about their domestic goings on? Their husbands are not there to listen to them. According to my estimate, with women aged 50 or younger, in full-time employment and with no young children to look after, 33% of them feel exasperated, and the figure shoots up to 50% among those women with young children. Children then become the victim of the bottled up stress. Child abuse as reported in Europe cannot be someone else's problem.

Assuming that people will be spending much longer time at home in the post-COVID world, what can we do to avoid tragic consequences such as the aforementioned "corona divorce"? It is important that we maintain stability on a day-to-day basis. My joint study indicates that the levels of emotional stresses such as exasperation, anxiety, and fear rose after the state of emergency was declared. There was, however, a group of people who remained unstirred—men who come from snowbound regions. For example, the number of people among the general population who felt "exasperation" increased by 7.5% from the first survey on March 13 to the third on April 10, with the declaration of the national state of emergency in between, whereas the increase among people in the snowy regions was by 4%. The increment rate is nearly half of the general population. These are individuals who inevitably spend many days inside their homes, locked in by heavy snowfalls. Their environment as such must have nurtured the resilience that is typical of these northern-country people. It being not a glorious personal attribute, but it goes a long way at times of enduring hardship.

We are, then, moving into an era when how to spend time at home becomes crucial. What would be the secret to making the hours at home more enjoyable? Would it solve the problem if both husband and wife have a job each and work from home? It would not work if the wife also has to busy herself keeping the household going while the husband locks himself in his room to work in the comfort of his insulated home office. I presented some evidence in Chap. 5 that pointed to the value of day-to-day conversations and domestic work-sharing in marriage. Why not try reducing the emotional distance with your partner? The solution is found in prudence and diligence before finding yourself in trouble.

Advice I could give would be this: I speak to all husbands working full time, do make a little time for your wives and let them unburden a little by listening to their worries and complaints. It might not go down very well in the beginning, but give it time and keep trying, then you will develop good skills in empathic listening. Then, you are moving one step forward. Some women might think this is not enough to make them happy. So, with a little bit of courage, say to your wife on a Sunday morning, "Let me join you and do some cleaning. I suppose the bathroom and toilets are the tough ones, I'll take care of them." This, of course, must be followed by your actual action. You do what you say, and soon you will find that your wife seems less distant than before and that your family life seems brighter.

"The Life" of Haruma Miura: "Economics of Duty and Sentiment" Personified

Actor Haruma Miura died.[2] Born in April 1990, he was merely 30 years and 3 months old. The news appeared on the media one Saturday afternoon when the second wave

---

[2] Haruma Miura was an up-and-coming actor who played, in 2016, one of the lead roles in a TV adaptation of *Never Let Me Go* by Kazuo Ishiguro. In theaters, he played Raskolnikov in

of COVID-19 was looming. The shock swept the nation; his last music video, Night Diver, was released posthumously and viewed online over 6 million times within 36 h.[3] TV news and shows ran features on him, and I, like many others, was struck not by his death, but by the life he had.

Three months or so before his death, he had published a self-produced book with a title *Nihonsei*, literally meaning "made in Japan."[4] By coincidence, I had my book, the original Japanese edition of this book, published at around the same time. My book was about the behavior of "humans with feelings" based mainly on Japanese studies, and I intended the book be also relevant to the readers of a remote future. Miura's book is based on the fieldwork which the actor himself conducted in all prefectures in Japan, visiting sites of local industries and interviewing people "in the field." Each of the articles about these places is accompanied by his essay under a subtitle, "Haruma's take on FUTURE and PRESERVATION." He writes variously about family bond, friendship between work colleagues, integration of modern technology, future of traditional industries, and so on from his personal viewpoints. I found that his *Made In Japan*—what he wrote as well as how he lived his life and the message he wanted to pass on—had so much in common with the main theme of my book. I want to explain how it is so.

An article about his book says, "Haruma Miura spent the last four years concerning himself with many 'industries' across Japan. *Nihonsei*, published immediately after his latest stage success, details local industries in each of 47 prefectures in Japan, taking these four years to visit each one of them and learn from the people who keep their traditions alive. ... Originally, this was a series of articles for a monthly magazine, but the work involved must have been disproportionate to a project as such in terms of the time and cost, as he made trips once a month, like ones he might do for location shooting, and moreover, he spent a substantial time researching in preparation for his interviews with local workers, artisans, etc. Despite all this, he continued this project for a whole four years, forty-eight months, covering the forty-seven locations, and interacting with everyday people. For what he has invested, he could have done dozens of TV location reports, and if those visits had an advertising agency involved, he would have made a substantial earning."

In economics terms, his dedication had too much cost against too little benefit. It tells me how much value he placed on promoting the virtues found in those local industries. He was known to have undergone a period of struggle in his early twenties, seriously considering of leaving the show business and taking up farming. I cannot imagine that it would be a decision to make lightly. In an interview he gave in 2010, he mentioned that he was "into cultivation." Perhaps, he recognized the value of being grounded, working hard physically as well as mentally without making a claim for it,

---

Dostoyevsky's *Crime and Punishment*, and Lola of *The Kinky Boots* when the Broadway musical ran a Japan tour.

[3] According to one interview, the actor enjoyed outdoor activities in his off time. The COVID-19 pandemic made it inevitable that a large part of work and life must be spent in confinement. One can only imagine that, being a single man, several months of self-confinement put an indescribable strain on his psychological wellbeing, which might have contributed to his death.

[4] Miura (2020).

and producing something meaningful for the time and effort dedicated to it. Contrary to his career of being in the limelight on spectacular stages, he had a deep-rooted longing for a down-to-earth life, living each day as humanely as possible.

Hamura Miura in his private life was deeply troubled in his late twenties. He was jotting down serious thoughts about life, about death, etc. in his notebook. With his work, however, he was building up a successful career, playing roles such as Raskolnikov of *Crime and Punishment* by Fyodor Dostoyevsky and Lola of the Broadway musical *Kinky Boots* with poignant, convincing performance. Aiming to expand his frontier to international stages, Haruma was studying English, as well. His own Japanese also became refined, more intelligent and insightful. We can witness it in the essays he wrote in his *Made In Japan* book, and one on Japanese lacquerware, in particular. He wrote,

> Natural lacquer comes from lacquer trees. It is collected by making scratches on the bark, which start to produce liquid resin. In a sense, it is like collecting the trees' blood. Those lacquer trees consume their lives to give us the raw material that is transformed into lacquerware, a piece of vessel that begins a new life as it is used and passed on.
>
> Actors shed tears at times in their performances. Tear, according to some source, is very close to blood in its composition. This makes me think that an actor could embody profound expressions and share the unforgettable emotional experience with the audience if he sublimates his whole, even his most painful memories.
>
> Lacquer trees are unloved trees, shunned and pushed away because of their toxicity. However, their blood, shed by making incisions into their bodies, have been for centuries useful to us, as adhesives, as sanitizer, and most of all, in artistic and historical objects, allowing us to develop cultural heritage. Lacquer trees are in fact so profound, awe-inspiring, and somewhat melancholic. I cannot help wishing that I could be a lacquer tree, for all those qualities attained by sacrificing one's own flesh and expressing with the whole being.[5]

The actor coined a term "aging enhancement of beauty" as opposed to aging effects of wear and tear, referring to the fact that lacquerware increases its charm and aesthetic quality through years of utilization.[6] Haruma Miura makes me think of Beethoven, Mozart, and other great composers that I described in Chap. 1. They all produced their masterpieces out of a period of great struggle in life,

The official sales copy of *Nihonsei* reads, "A book that takes you on a journey through Haruma Miura's viewpoints to consider what 'Japan' should look like in the future." In the book, Miura poses a question, "Have you ever done anything for the world in 50 years' time?" The readers will remember that, in Chap. 3, I pointed out the problem with the hometown tax donation scheme. It is turning into an online shopping system where people just purchase "thank-you gifts" based on the monetary gain they can make against the items' market value, quite irrespective of the background information about these local specialties. As a result, the cultural value of these items and sentimental attachment to "hometowns" are being neglected. Miura's project was at the opposite end of this trend. As the world headed toward an AI-powered dry society, he cherished the narratives about local crafts and the people

---

[5] Miura (2020: 31).

[6] There is a colloquial phrase equivalent to "wear and tear" in Japanese, but its antonym does not exist in the Japanese dictionary.

who produced them. He wanted to promote their value and pass it on to our future generations.

He was saying, "Show business is not all about glitz and fun. I can be a medium to communicate messages like 'war dehumanizes,' 'discrimination should not be tolerated,' and so on." In Chap. 2, , I described how non-Japanese people exposed to the modern culture of Japan in their countries developed affinity with the Japanese and the readiness to accept them in their workplaces or communities. Pursuing this course of action to promote Japanese culture may help to improve international relations. I imagine that Miura was aware of this potential responsibility of the cultural media, such as films and TV dramas. As I mentioned before, he was learning foreign languages and proactively seeking opportunities beyond his own country.

On his last public appearance, he said, "I firmly believe that the entertainment industry is full of humanity. I sincerely hope that this humanizing profession will contribute one day to uplift everyone's morale and give them hopes."[7] The actor devoted his entire being to make the stage productions he was involved in "full of humanity" so that it encouraged people and stayed in their memories. In this sense, the project for his book was, perhaps, his pilgrimage to Japanese industries to find an answer for himself, what he could do so that his acting work, those various productions, become an "industry" that is firmly rooted in people's domestic lives.

He was trying to improve the part of his life that does not come under a spotlight. Speaking in an interview about his future focus as an actor, he said, "It's to live better as a human being. I think it will help to lead a life better in many ways, so I can keep the inner peace as days go, which will hopefully allow me to do my job properly." Quoting the legendary actress Kirin Kiki, he also said "True that 'an actor must be able to truly understand the pain in a person, their feelings, their desires, and empathize with them.' I believe in the possibility to make something truly awesome out of the current production if all cast members really communicated with and support each other through our respective roles." He was a reserved and considerate person in work as well as in private. Assuming that he had many peers and rivals who were assertive egoists, what made it possible that this selfless actor who puts his co-casts before himself became such a leading-role player with a palpable presence?

I think it was his aspiration to make the best not only of himself but of the stage as a whole. If the overall performance was less than satisfactory, it would ultimately devalue theatrical entertainment in general. The implication of this would be an eventual decline of his and other actors' work. It is therefore most important, from a broad and long-term perspective, to ensure the production be closer to perfection. This will require each participant to have confidence in others and enable the team to work in perfect synchronicity, thereby boosting the morale on the floor. Miura, appearing in a cooking program for an online video, suggested that he would be interested to learn something he could cook for the crew of the current production he was in "to boost the motivation on the floor." Here is a man who places himself among others and makes an effort to play his part. Everyone around him knows how

---

[7] His own words from a comment he made at the last stage performance.
Distributed at 17:00, Wednesday, July 22, 2020.

hard he tries for it. At the same time, he is a generous person, whose big smile warms up people around him, like sunshine does. Someone like him is loved, trusted, and accepted to be a leader. In Chap. 1, I explained the importance of the "virtuous cycle" mechanism to enhance trust relationships in the workplace, etc. Haruma Miura was enacting the leader that enabled the virtuous cycle.

In the last live talk show that he broadcast from his home, Miura was smiling, seemingly enjoying himself, and also very caring. There was a moment when he put a question to his guest personalities—other casts of his last stage production—his face had a serious air. The question was, regarding his future path, "which should I go to, stage or film, and what would be a desirable character to play?" He waited for answers silently. It seemed to me that the question had always been in his mind as he underwent a transformation from an ambivalent young man to a mature adult. The more I found out about this young actor, the more I could visualize his way of life, that he learned and absorbed knowledge from various sources and tried to build on it for his future. He was learning Chinese and English, and his Japanese becoming more refined, precise and intelligent. He was learning about science, medicine, etc. in an effort to enrich his work and life. Most of these facts came to my knowledge after his death. He was a precious gem that people of all kinds and generations loved unconditionally, only realizing it when he is already lost. The way in which he lived his life is full of insights into the way of life we would need to adopt in order to survive and live well in the coming post-COVID era.

The late Taro Okamoto, an artist whom I admire, once said in relation to the fire at Horyuji Temple in 1949 that burned down most part of the national treasure ancient fresco painting:

> Lamenting does not solve anything. ... A more fundamental and immediate issue is elsewhere. We only have to *be* Horyuji Temple.

I wonder, perhaps, we can be Haruma Miura; to be supportive as he was; to never forget smiling as he never did; and to appreciate each and every day as he did. We only have to start from where we can. I imagine it would put that brilliant smile on his face and make him happy up in heaven to hear us say,

> Lamenting does not solve anything. We only have to *be* Haruma Miura ourselves.

The Postponement of the 2020 Olympic Games and Ninjo the Humanity

A decision was made that the Tokyo 2020 Olympic and Paralympic Games scheduled for July 2020 be postponed due to the COVID-19 pandemic. The Games has an extensive impact on various industries. The tourism and restaurant industries, in particular, will be handling a surge of demand as people from across the world flock to Japan. The postponement means that these industries suffer considerable damage to their economic profits.

During the bidding process for the 2020 Olympic Games, Japan made its presentation with an emphasis on its tourism and food service industries that they would provide international visitors with comprehensive hospitality in a particularly Japanese way, labeling it "omotenashi." Since the Games was officially accorded to Tokyo, these industries have invested in horning up their competence and expertise in the "omotenashi" hospitality services. Thus, for the convenience of the discourse on this topic, I will use "the omotenashi industry" as an umbrella label for tourism, restaurant, and other food service industries.

People working in the omotenashi industry surely enjoy economic benefits by offering services of a hospitable nature, but presumably, they also derive joy out of providing generous, hospitable services, or simply being nice to other people. Assuming this, what factors are at work in the postponement to generate a sense of unhappiness among these people in the omotenashi industry?

The economic damage due to COVID-19 surely extends to other industries, too. For the omotenashi industry people, it must be particularly shocking that all the invested efforts went to waste. I suspect that this shock is not entirely attributed to economic loss alone. Is it possible that their happiness levels are lowered due to the sense of loss attributed to the lost opportunities to render their hospitable services? I explored this point using the data I gathered.

The postponement of Tokyo 2020 was officially announced on March 24. As it has been mentioned, I conducted a series of survey to analyze the impact of COVID-19 after cases of infection were confirmed in Japan. The questionnaire was administered to the same people every time, so that the data allowed to follow up longitudinal changes. Figure 6.1 shows the cumulative COVID-19 confirmed cases, with the markings for the dates of three survey sessions (March 10, March 27, and April 10) and the announcement of Tokyo 2020 postponement (March 24).

The first survey was conducted when Japan was only beginning to see the effects of the pandemic, and no major administrative measures were in place except the temporary closure of schools. The postponement of the Games was announced just before the second survey, so the data will reflect its impact. The third survey was administered after the declaration of the national state of emergency. It is highly possible that people were under considerable strain socially and economically. It is therefore supposed that the data on the economic impact is greater at the third survey than the second, while the negative implication of the Olympic Games being postponed is not alleviated; meanwhile, the psychological shock is great at the time of the second survey, but it subsides at the time of the third session.

Figure 6.2. illustrates the fluctuation of happiness levels over the three survey sessions. Figure 6.2a is based on the data of the segment of respondents who considered the probability of the Games going ahead was lower than 40% in the first survey. Those who considered the same probability to be more than 60% at the time of the first survey are reflected in Fig. 6.2b. Both charts are organized in comparison between two subgroups: one representing the omotenashi industry workers and the other representing those working in other industries.

Figure 6.2a shows that the happiness levels of omotenashi workers are low from the beginning and remain constantly low. An interesting observation is that their

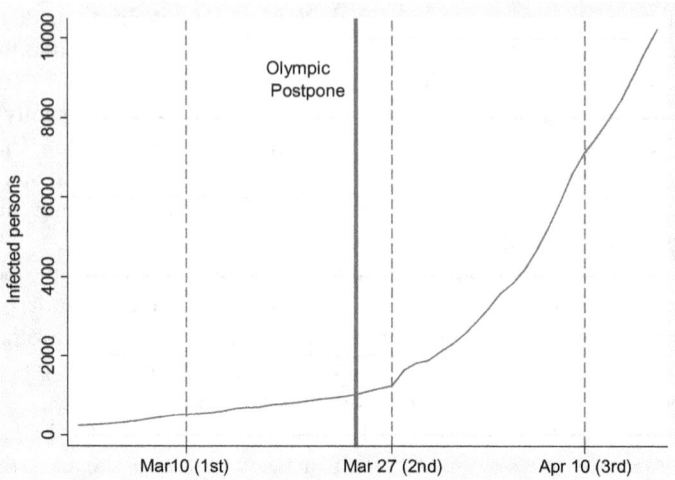

Fig. 6.1 Timing of surveys and postponement of Olympic Games. *Note* The curved line indicates the total number of infected persons. The thick solid line indicates the date of the announcement of postponing the Olympics. The dashed lines indicate the time points of Waves 1 (March 10), 2 (March 27), and 3 (April 10)

happiness levels are almost unaffected by the postponement of the Games or the state of national emergency contrary to the perceived relevance of these events to their industry. By contrast, the other people were feeling incrementally unhappy as time elapsed. This can be interpreted that these non-omotenashi workers suffered significant economic losses due to the spread of COVID-19, which diminished their levels of happiness.

The happiness levels among the omotenashi workers were consistent while those of others dramatically decreased. The former's happiness levels were much lower than those of their counterpart at first, but consequently this was reversed.

We can see in Fig. 6.2b that the happiness level of the omotenashi workers is a little higher than that of others' in the first survey, but it dramatically drops in the second survey, far below the happiness level of the others. At the time of the third survey, their level of happiness recovered to almost level with the other group of people. By contrast, the happiness levels of the "others" group constantly decline, just like we saw in Fig. 6.2a. This suggests that the non-omotenashi workers' happiness levels decreased corresponding to the increase of the negative economic impact and irrespective of the postponement of Tokyo 2020.

We can therefore summarize the above as follows: the happiness levels of people who work in the omotenashi industry vary considerably depending on the levels of their expectation for the Games to take place. Those who had high expectations are hit hard by the postponement, significantly lowering their happiness levels, but this effect weakens in about two weeks. Given the apparent recovery of the happiness levels despite the increasing economic losses, this recovery is possibly attributable

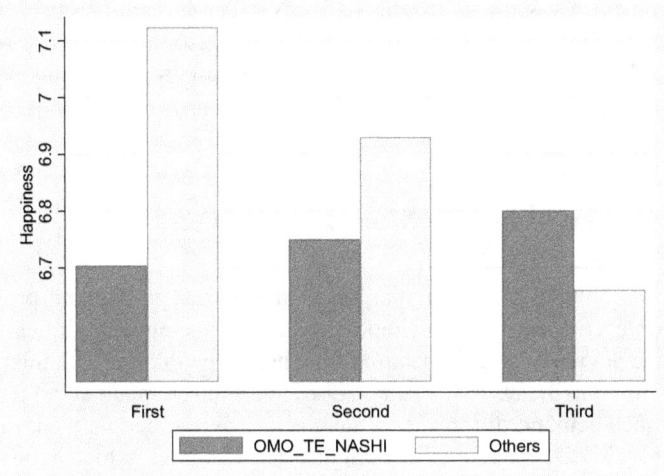

(a) Low expectation group

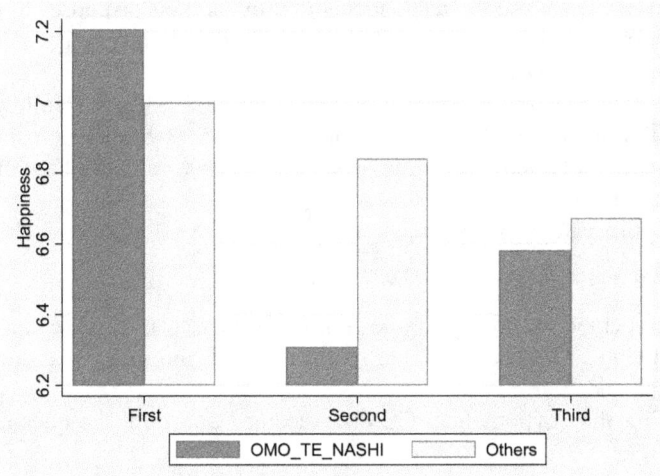

(b) High expectation group

Fig. 6.2 Happiness levels

to the disappointment about losing the opportunity to engage in hospitable services. These observations lead to the following:

> workers with a hospitality mindset derive a sense of happiness from the act of providing hospitality.

This statement gives us an insight that people derive happiness from work not only in terms of the economic benefits it brings, but also the joy of engaging in the work itself. This is the secret of Japanese "omotenashi" that enchants people from all over the world.

Life and Money, Which Is More Important?

In this section, I will present an analysis of the dataset mentioned previously, to examine people's decision-making about purchasing insurance in critical situations. The insurance demand varies depending on whether people are risk tolerant or risk averse. Risk tolerant means that a person does not mind so much about having risks, so the insurance demand diminishes, whereas risk averse people want to minimize the risks, for which they opt for taking out insurance policies, which in turn raises the insurance demand. The question we ask is, how does the insurance demand fluctuate as COVID-19 spreads?

In the survey, we asked the respondents to provide their responses to two sets of hypothetical questions, one about a "hypothetical non-life insurance" and the other a "hypothetical COVID vaccine."

The first "hypothetical non-life insurance" question asked the following: "You have 100,000 yen (approx. 1,000 USD), and there is a 50% chance of losing it. There is an insurance available to cover the loss. How much would you be willing to pay for the premium?"

Eleven options are provided:

from 1 (zero yen) to 11 (more than 50,000 yen).

A prudent person would pay for the premium if there was a 50% chance of losing the 1,000 dollars. The need to minimize the risk of monetary loss increases the insurance demand.

Concerning the "hypothetical COVID vaccine" question, the question goes as follows:

"A vaccine has been created and verified to be effective against the novel coronavirus, and it is available at the cost of 100,000 yen, but this is not covered by insurance. Would you pay the cost and have yourself vaccinated?" Then, five options are provided:

from 1 (definitely not) to 5 (absolutely, yes).

If the respondents valued their lives, they would choose to have the vaccine. The need for avoiding death increases the demand for the vaccine.

Given this context, we analyzed the data, and the results are shown in Figs. 6.3 and 6.4. Both charts are organized in gender comparison, showing the results from the three survey sessions. Previous research suggests that, in general, women are known to be more risk averse than men are.[8] On the basis of this observation, we

---

[8] Gneezy and List (2014).

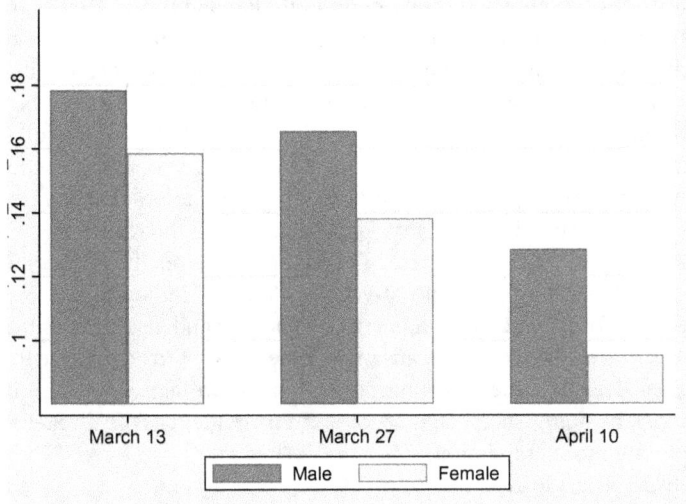

Fig. 6.3 Change of insurance demand as COVID-19 spread. *Note* The interval represents the 95% confidence intervals

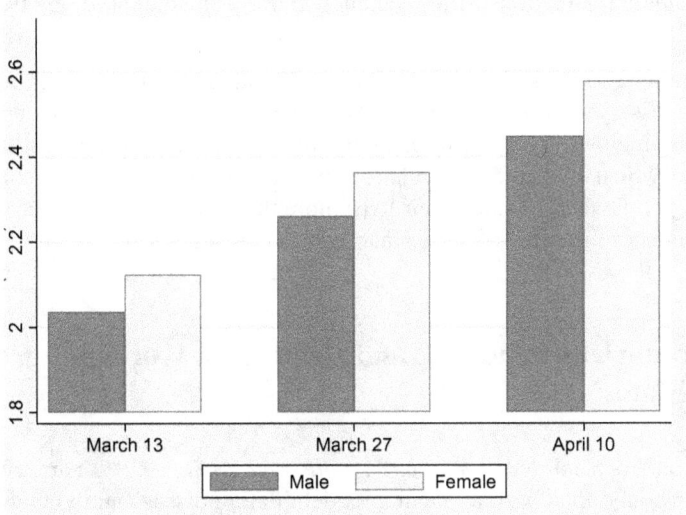

Fig. 6.4 Change of vaccine demand as COVID-19 spreads. *Note* The interval represents the 95% confidence intervals

predict that values are higher for women in both demand types. However, Figs. 6.3 shows that, with respect to the insurance demand, the results defy our prediction. Men indicate higher insurance demand levels than women, suggesting that men are more incentivized to minimize the risk of losing money. Furthermore, the insurance demand declines as the COVID-19 situation is exacerbated. This indicates that the urge to reduce the risk of monetary loss is weakening. It is understandable that a critical situation turns a person defiant and more risk tolerant. However, women being more risk tolerant than men, this goes right against the results of conventional economic studies. Why is this the case? Let us turn to the results of vaccine demand.

Figures 6.4, illustrating the trend of vaccine demand, indicates that women have stronger demand for the vaccine than men do. The demand also rises as the COVID-19 situation is exacerbated. This means that women have a stronger urge to minimize the risk to their lives than men. Furthermore, men and women alike, their inclination to avoid the risk by being vaccinated becomes more evident as the threat to their lives is perceived with more conviction.

These observations lead to the following:

(1) women place less importance than men on financial losses in life-threatening situations; financial loss is deprioritized at a greater risk to life, and
(2) women place more importance than men on preserving their lives in life-threatening situations; life becomes more valuable at a greater risk to life.

From these, a conclusion is drawn: a person's financial resources are finite, which makes it necessary to measure the cost of securing funds against the cost of preserving a life; economizing the cost of insuring the fund increases a reserve for the cost of life-saving, which is a trade-off relationship; as the threat to life becomes more imminent, people tend to value their lives more than their money; therefore, fear of death diminishes the value of money and boosts the value of life.

The Coronavirus Pandemic and Healthcare Workers' Mental States

A nonfiction story entitled *A banana? At this time of night?* is a narrative about a wheelchair-bound man with an incurable, debilitating disease and young volunteer carers, and the story revolves around their day-to-day interactions. The film adaptation featured Yo Oizumi for the principal character and Haruma Miura as a young medical student, one of the volunteer carers. The man in wheelchair was having everything his own way, and the medical student takes care of him to the best of his ability, but this young, sensitive student has something that troubles him, so one day, he declares that he has had enough of both studying and volunteering. The selfish man in wheelchair lectures him, but this changes the young man's mind, and he resumes his pursuits. Several years later, the student has become a medical doctor, practicing in a rural town somewhere. He looks up at the sky, reminiscing over the selfish, disabled man, who is now dead. The film ends with Haruma Miura's smile. The picture is somewhat dreamlike, with a lot of light and in an impressionist composition. The rock music played in the film goes "It's awesome to be alive…" matching the underlying theme of the story—it's dazzling how wonderful life is.

The film was shot in Sapporo, Hokkaido. Phone calls from a public telephone of the 1980s, scenes of sun-lit outdoor in fresh summer green, the campus of Hokkaido University, and people speaking with the local accent—here and there the film is embellished with the things that are so familiar to me. The images bring back memories, of the past that will never come back. My uncle, who died forty years ago, studied medicine in Sapporo and used to practice in a small town somewhere in Hokkaido. The young medical student in the film, dressed in a somewhat old-fashioned style, reminded me of my late uncle, whose life was not quite straightforward.

In the present surge of COVID-19, healthcare workers are the ones who are exposed to the highest risk of catching the disease. Moreover, slander and a discriminatory attitude are directed at these workers and their families, which has turned into a social phenomenon.[9] They must be under considerable psychological stress because of these risks of infection and discrimination in society. However, if these key workers who are fighting COVID-19 in the frontline become mentally worn out, the quality of medical care will suffer, and by extension, the disease will further spread and cause more damage. In this sense, this is a grave socioeconomic problem. I therefore examined the psychological impact of COVID-19 with a focus on healthcare workers, using the survey data collected during the pandemic period.

Figure 6.5 shows the trend of new confirmed cases between March 1 and June 2, 5 dates of surveys (thin solid lines), and the start (thick solid line) and end (thick dashed line) of the state of emergency period. The third survey was administered three days after the state of emergency was declared (March 27). The threat of COVID-19 was most strongly felt around this date as the new cases of infection peaked at this point in the survey period. The fourth survey was conducted during the state of emergency period, and the fifth and final survey was about two weeks after the declaration of the state of emergency was lifted. The case numbers dropped to an extent at the time of the fourth survey, but the state of emergency was still imposed, and the general mood in society was of nervous alert. The fifth survey took place when the case numbers were low and the state of emergency had already been removed, so people were not as alert as they had been.

Given these contexts, a comparison before and after the outbreak can be made from the data of the second and third surveys, while the data of surveys four and five serve for the comparison between the time under and after the state of emergency.

One of the questions in the survey is about the respondents' happiness levels, that they rate how happy they feel at the time on a scale of 1 (not happy) to 11 (happy).

---

[9] For example, nurseries refused entry to children of healthcare workers in the name of precautionary measures, necessitating these workers to stay home or take leaves, and in some cases, lose their jobs.
Source: Babazono, A. of Kyushu University, *Discrimination against Healthcare Workers: how should we face the fear and anxiety about novel coronavirus disease?*, June 24, 2020, https://www.jcer.or.jp/blog/babazonoakira20200624.html.

120   6 What Came Out of the Spread of COVID-19?

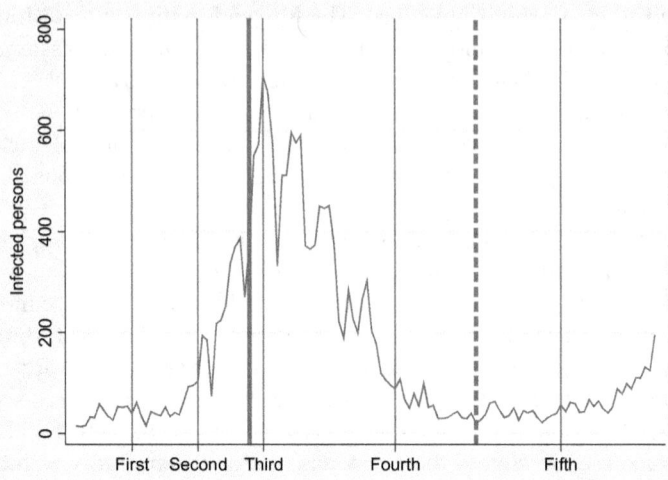

Fig. 6.5 Changes in daily COVID-19 infections in Japan, March 1 to July 2. *Note* The surveys were conducted on March 10 and 27, April 10, May 8, and June 12. These dates are marked with thin lines in Fig. 6.5. The thick solid line indicates the day the Japanese government declared the state of emergency (April 7), and the thick dashed line marks the end of the emergency period (May 25). *Source* The daily confirmed infection case numbers were taken from the Ministry of Health, Labour and Welfare official website: https://www.mhlw.go.jp/stf/covid-19/open-data.html (accessed July 4, 2020)

Figure 6.6 illustrates the average scores from each session. The scores of healthcare workers are shown in dark bars, and other workers in light ones. Both groups show the highest scores in the first survey, and there is not much difference between the two groups. The scores continue to drop up to the third session, with healthcare workers showing a particularly sharp decline. This is a reflection of the considerable stress to which these workers are subjected, far greater than other workers.

A curious difference is observed between healthcare workers and the others after this point. The happiness levels hit the lowest at the time of the third survey, then those of healthcare workers bounces back in the subsequent session while the levels remain unchanged among other workers. This may be explained by the outbreak being curtailed that healthcare workers were relieved of some of the stress. Whereas, other workers were not feeling happier than before because the lockdown continued under the state of emergency, and they still had to deal with various restrictions in life. Meanwhile, the trend of happiness levels between sessions four and five is again different: those of healthcare workers do not change, and other workers show a relative increase. This increase may be a reflection of the regained freedom in social activities, but relaxing restrictions on the behavior of the public comes with the risk of allowing COVID-19 to flare up again, causing a second wave of outbreak. Healthcare workers know this too well (in fact, the second wave did occur two weeks after this survey), and the anxiety and alertness add to their stress, hence no reduction of stress. Furthermore, not much seems to have changed in society in terms of the

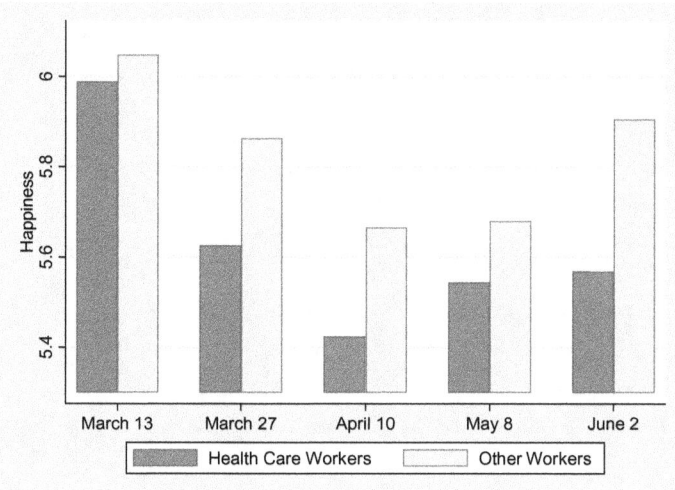

Fig. 6.6 Mean values of happiness levels

lack of understanding and discriminatory attitude toward those workers. Therefore, the happiness levels of healthcare workers do not improve but stay at a low level.

The above observations reveal the nature of COVID-19:

> the pandemic exposes healthcare workers to considerable stress more than to other people, and it is not easy to recover from the stressful conditions.

These are the people who fight in the frontier to protect us and our society. It is important that society offers sympathetic support to them and makes sure that they do not break down because of the stress. This is the lesson learned from the coronavirus pandemic that we as a society must share.

On July 18, the second wave of the pandemic hit Tokyo. It was also the day I learned of the death of the young actor Haruma Miura. I was thrown into a reverie—the young medical student that I saw in the film becomes projected over the actor in real life, and vague memories from decades ago come back to life, the moment when I learned of the unexpected passing of my uncle. Being merely a schoolboy, I was confronted by the meaning of life for the first time in my life. I was deep in my thoughts. Time froze. It took me a few days to process the profundity of the event, but finally the roaring of summer cicadas brought me back.

Chapter 7
Concluding Chapter How Can Community Be Rational?

> There are a good side and bad to a community life. You are obliged to do favors or be nice to your neighbors all the time, you know....

The man is taking a yoga pose, his legs crossed and the torso twisted 45 degrees, facing me, as he answered my question, which was about how he managed with the people in the neighborhood. In the summer of 1993, I was in Egypt. I was visiting Cairo with a group of backpackers, staying in an apartment in the city. The man is Machi Tanaka, a Japanese travel writer and a tenant of this apartment. He lived here with his wife. This generous man was in his thirties, and we young backpackers in our twenties looked up to him like a big brother. In the room, there was a photograph showing a home party with many backpackers. Among them was one of my classmates from year 1 at university. "Kazu, he was a funny guy, a good man," said Machi. I realized that Waseda University had quite a few odd ones like me.

He was preparing for a research trip, and one of us was going to look after the apartment while he was away. The instructions he gave were quite thorough, including how often his plants had to be watered. This man, being a freelancer, seemed to be making a reasonable income from creative work to maintain a good standard of life. He showed us some of his work—travel magazines with beautiful photographs and articles, which seemed interesting. I saw a paperback in English on his desk, next to an English-Japanese dictionary and a notepad. He said that he had a translation job for the first time, and that he was working two or three pages a day. It was Graham Hancock's *The Signs and the Seal: A Quest for the Lost Ark of the Covenant*, and according to him, it was like George Lucas and Steven Spielberg's *Raiders of the Lost Ark*.[1] I asked him more about his life in Cairo. He gave me some examples, like that traveling minstrels would turn up during fetes, and it was customary to tip them for their performance. The question I mentioned above at the outset was a part of this conversation.

---

[1] The Japanese translation of *Fingerprints of the Gods* was published in 1996 and became a bestseller.

The Mediterranean sea trade of the Middle Ages was dominated by Maghrebi traders, who held the uncontested authority in the region. According to Avner Greif, their success is explained as follows[2]: despite the vast area covered and the distances between remote ports, the Maghrebi traders maintained a closely-knit web of peer traders, forming a particularly exclusive community based on their long-standing, close personal relationships. They shared a private code of conduct (unofficial rules of trade) amongst themselves, and anyone who disrespected it to make profits would be cast out as word spread throughout the community. This would mean an absolute rejection from any future trade for good. Breaching the code of conduct for an immediate gain will result in a loss of the profit that would have been derived from the trade on a long term. Everyone knew this, and no one would dare. The Maghrebi traders conducted business without much trouble on this retaliation-based relationship of trust and made a major economic success. However, their reign did not last very long. The rise of Genoese traders soon replaced Maghrebis and took over the Mediterranean sea trade. These merchants operated on the basis of official trade rules. Violators were tried and penalized in court. It was a law enforcing authority that regulated the trade, rather than collective coercion. Their system allowed anyone to take part in trade in the area without necessarily having a long-standing connection with particular players. It meant a freedom to choose who to trade with to maximize profits without being restricted to usual customers. This system made it possible to generate more profit from trade by attracting more participants. In modern economics terms, the market mechanism enabled their economic growth. While the economy based on a web of trust that was formed by close, involved relationships can facilitate economic gain, the market economy could generate far greater gain. Noting that Greif meant by "trust relationship" one that is formed between individuals who pursue their own interest, and not a form of connections based on sympathy, his argument suggests that obligation in relationships has some advantages. However, what is not mentioned is the fact that the obligating relationship always comes with a shrewd aspect, and he leaves out in his argument that close, involved relationships may restrict individual's freedom in the day-to-day contexts outside a trade relationship.

In 2014, I was taking part in a behavioral economics conference held at Keio University. The venue was in a brand-new south-wing building near the main gates of the Mita campus.[3] At the building entrance, there was a panel with details of the conference, and there was another next to it, for a cultural workshop open to the general public. Something in it caught my eyes—the lecturer was Mr. Machi Tanaka! I sneaked in the workshop during a break of the conference, and there he was. He had not changed much on the outside after some twenty years. The room was scented with the smell of incense that came from the Middle East. On the wall, photographs were projected, showing the life in beautiful Syria before the country

---

[2] Greif (2009).

[3] The classroom had a brilliant contrast of retro and modern, the former being age-old desks and chairs. These have been serving students generation after generation from the era of Showa, since the mid-1920s. They represent the history of learning students at this university. Many of its students come from wealthy families, and these fortunate young people can afford many things. To my mind, this is part of the reason why the university values the things money cannot buy.

7 Concluding Chapter How Can Community Be Rational?

was consumed by political unrest, followed by a video clip, in which some traveling minstrels played lively music in a festival in Cairo, about twenty years before. Tanaka returned to Japan after eight years in Cairo, and his main line of work was still in writing. I briefly spoke to him during a short break. He was surprised to see me as I reminded him that I visited him in Cairo about twenty years before. Later that day, I wrote him an email, thanking him for his generosity that I enjoyed as a young man. I added that his words, which I presented at the outset of this chapter, stayed with me and were relevant to my research interest. In his reply, he wrote:

> Those days, I was tired of the exhausting community life of Egypt. I fear that I must have come across as a gloomy pessimist. ... Every day was prone to some troubles, things were never done without a hitch, and you faced atrocious envy and jealousy. ...
>
> But seeing the current state of Japanese society, where not causing others trouble has gone too far to prohibit helping one another, I sometimes feel a little nostalgic about those days in Cairo.

It echoed with the problem of which I am aware today as an economist. Just like his words became inscribed in my backpacker consciousness twenty years ago and led me to the research I pursue today, these words that came from him twenty years on will stay with me as an economist for another twenty years. Back in Fukuoka, I went to a bookstore to find a copy of his books. I found one in the travel section. I opened the cover, and there it was: his profile that read "Bachelor's degree conferred by the Faculty of Economics, Keio University."

Epilogue

In 2019, Chief Cabinet Secretary Suga is on a TV screen, making a national announcement, "The new imperial era will be named Reiwa." A deja-vu moment. Witnessing a start of a new era, and yet, my mind traveled back 31 years, when I heard this phrase for the first time—"The new imperial era is named Heisei." Mr. Suga then took the office of prime minister the following year. History repeats itself. The beginning of a new era made me think poignantly of my life that already crossed two eras. The Showa era was a time when behaviors based on the bonding through indebtedness and fellow feeling were palpable. The subsequent Heisei era seems to me to have lost this humanity side to some extent. I must keep watching how the trend may turn out in the new Reiwa Japan.

Photo of Yoshihide Suga holding up a frame with the new imperial era, "Reiwa". © JIJI Press, Ltd.

As a boy, I used to enjoy daydreaming. In a class at school, my mind was elsewhere, exploring the most captivating world in my head, which was almost toxic, I enjoyed it too much. But I was not gifted in expressing in words, written or spoken, so the great fun of my inner, imaginary world could not be shared with friends. Such was my childhood—a dull child. I somehow managed to make it to university, and then went on to spend several years trotting about in the wide world as a budget backpacker.

Then, out of sheer luck, I became a researcher. Yet again, I was drawn to niche topics and quirky subjects, and no one in my circle of economists was even remotely interested in my research. My tutorial classes were my idea show in disguise, testing my research ideas on students. Still, I had many wonderful encounters and found a few fellow researchers across the world with shared interest. One day, I received an email from Ms. Kazuko Yahagi, an editor of a publishing house, the Toyo Keizai Inc. She contacted me after reading an article I had written for a newspaper for the first time. Her email contained the following message:

> ... The subject is one of our major fields of interest, and I have always been keen to find insightful cases in Japan. ... Would it be possible for us to meet next time you come to Tokyo, perhaps, for an academic conference?

I gathered that this was an invitation, if very indirect, to write a book. With a shadow of a doubt lingering in the back of my mind, I nonetheless sent her a reply, listing my ideas for a book, together with a working title that came to my mind. Strike while the iron is hot, as they say. This is how it all started, and I have come to publish my first ever single-author book. This is a result culminated from the support I had from so many people along the way, from those eventful student days, through the period of countless rejections of papers submitted to international journals.

I would like to acknowledge my gratitude, first of all, to the late Professor Yujiro Hayami, who guided me to the world of research; Professor Keijiro Otsuka, who so generously offered his supervision for my Ph.D. at the Graduate School of Tokyo Metropolitan University; and Professor Sonobe, who was a co-researcher in a joint research project with Professor Otsuka. These last two professors have taught me all there is to know about conducting a research project, writing up a paper, and getting it published. I am deeply indebted to them, for if not for them, it would have been impossible for me to see this day. I would also like to thank Professor Seki Asano, who taught me econometrics and was an examiner of my Ph.D. thesis; economists Yasuyuki Sawada and Yasuyuki Todo, who were prominent young researchers when I was still an economist in the making, and who are always generous to impart invaluable insights to my research-related questions; my colleagues from the Graduate School, Tomoya Matsumoto and Yukichi Mano, and Professor Shin Inyong, who kindly answered my questions that I could not bring to the star economists. I am deeply indebted, for these individuals' support was invaluable for me to make it through the post graduate years, the toughest and most grueling time of my life.

I am also indebted to my co-researchers Yoshiro Tsutsui and Fumio Otake, for their inspiring discussions that make me realize the importance of narratives in research; economists Charles Yuji Horioka and Shinsuke Ikeda, generous colleagues who show great interest in my research topics, and economist Masao Ogaki, whose ideas about economy and Christianity are always inspiring. My special thanks also go to my international colleagues with whom I have had the honor of pursuing joint research, including Alison Booth, Nattavudh Powdthavee, Russel Smyth, and Fabio Sabatini. I thank all others, too, for their kind support on various terms to make my research possible. For publishing this book in English, Charles Yuji Horioka provided me with his expert knowledge, and so did the translation team at Simul International, Inc. and Springer editor Junno-Kawakami.

I have been fortunate to have support from the following non-economist people, too, to whom I am grateful: Alison Booth, physicist Tomohiro Sasamoto, Felidae expert Akihiro Yamane, and travel writer Machi Tanaka, who kindly fact-checked the sections that concerned them, and a fourth year student in my tutorial class, Naoya Oishi, and an economics student Takashige Masuyama, who read my manuscript and gave me their feedback from non-specialist points of view.

In the first meeting with the editor Kazuko Yahagi, I told her that I had about three years in mind to finish writing this book. It was December 2018. It is not a secret that I had no idea what it took to write a book, but I soon found myself on a right track once my pen started rolling. And come the new year, in January, my backpacker spontaneity got the better of me, and I was making a request to her that my book be published much sooner. "Certainly." Her response was crisp, and suddenly the whole thing seemed so real. I am so grateful for her efforts to bring this book of a first-time author into the world.

When a regnal year changes, this gives me the impression that society is going to be transformed. As the eras move on, people come and go, generations over generations. It is possible that my grandchildren will be born into the next era after Reiwa, and there is little doubt that this would be the case for their children. It is inevitable that times change and so do people. However, empirical studies in economics have shown that certain aspects of human perception and cognition survive and continue stimulating the economy and impacting society.[1] Then, there is the rise of artificial intelligence, the most remarkable development in human history. Will the sentimental humanity of people remain to be a driving force in human society? This humanity aspect that I refer to as *"giri ninjo"* is a hot topic in frontier research as much as it is a concept so familiar to humankind for centuries.

Finally, I would like to tell my parents Akio and Hiroko, my wife Mafumi, and my daughters Beniha and Nina that "I love you." And a final message to my grandchildren and great-grandchildren, who are yet to be born and will one day read this: your grandpa (or great-grandpa) was thinking about you while writing this, and would be very happy to have your feedback.

---

[1] See, for example, Algan and Cahuc (2010).

References

Literature in Japanese

Arai, Noriko. 2018. *AI vs. kyokasho ga yomenai kodomotachi* [AI vs. children who cannot read school textbooks]. Toyo Keizai Inc.
Doume, Takuo. 2008. *Adam Smith, Doutoku-kanjouron to Fukokuron no sekai* [Adam Smith, the theory of moral sentiment and the wealth of nations]. Chuokoron-Shinsha, Inc.
Fujisawa, Moto. 2012. *Daijobu, shinumade ikiru gouchi Fujisawa Hideyuki Burai no saigo* [Don't worry, I will live till I die—the go player Fujisawa Hideyuki: the last days of the rascal]. Kadokawa Shoten.
Fujiwara, Masahiko. 2005. *Kokka no hinkaku* [The dignity of nation state]. Shinchosha.
Hayami, Yujiro. 2000. *Shinban, Kaihatsu keizaigaku, Shokokumin no hinkon to tomi* [New edition, Developmental economics, the world's poverty and wealth]. Soubunsha.
Inose, Naoki. 2010. *Showa 16-nen natsu no haisen* [The defeat in Summer, the year 16 of Showa]. Chuokoron-Shinsha, Inc.
Kameda, Tatsuya. 2017. *Moraru no kigen: jikken-syakaikagaku karano toi* [The origin of morality: a question from the perspective of experimental social sciences]. Iwanami Shoten, Publishers.
Kandori, Michihiro. 2014. *Mikurokeizaigaku no chikara* [The power of microeconomics]. Nippon Hyoron Sha Co., Ltd. Publishers.
Kimura, Sota (ed.). 2018. *AI jidai no kenpo-ron: Jinkouchinou ni jinken wa aruka* [Constitutional arguments in the AI era: does AI deserve human rights?]. Mainichi Shimbun Publishing Inc.
Kobayashi, Keiichiro. 2018. Keizai seicho to atarashii keiyaku [Economic growth and new contract]. In *Zaisei hatan-go: Kiki no shinario bunseki* [Post-economic-collapse: Scenario analysis of crisis], ed. Keiichiro Kobayashi. Nikkei Inc.
Miura, Haruma. 2020. *Nihon-sei* [Made in Japan]. Wani Books Inc.
Nishimura, Kazuo. 2006. *Man'in-onrei, Keizaigaku nandemo onayami-sodanjo* [Full-house, All-purpose solicitor of economics]. Nikkei Inc.
Sasaki, Masaru. 2011. "Chingin wa donoyouni kimarunoka: Soboku na gimon ni kotaeru" [How are wages determined?: A simple question]. *Japan Labor Review* 611: 4–13.
Shimazawa, Manabu. 2019. Zaisei un'ei taishugeigou sakeyo 100-cho-en yosan o tou (ge) Keizai kyoshitsu [National budget management must not give in to public opinions—questioning the 100T yen budget (second part) Economics lesson]. *Nihon Keizai Shimbun*, January 23, 2019: 24.
Tan, Michio. 2017. *Why does Fujisoba pay bonuses to part-timers?* Shueisya Inc.
Yamanaka, Shinya, Seiji Hirao, and Keiko Hirao. 2017. *Yujo, Hirao Seiji to Yamanaka Shinya 'saigo no ichinen'* [Friendship, the 'last one year' between Seiji Hirao and Shinya Yamanaka]. Kodansha Ltd.

Yamamura, Eiji. 2018. Furusato nozei minaoshi e, ritateki douki no koudou sonchou o, genten kaiki, henreihin kinshi ga suji, Keizai kyoshitsu [Hometown tax donation in review, philanthropic motivation must be acknowledged, return to the original purpose, it is right to ban thank-you gifts, Economics lesson]. *Nihon Keizai Shimbun*, October 8, 2018: 24.

Translated Literature

Acemoglu, Daron, and James A. Robinson. 2013. *Kokka wa Naze Suitai surunoka: Kenryoku, Han-ei, Hinkon no Kigen Ge-kan* [Why nations fail] 2012, trans. Shinobu Onizawa. Hayakawa Publishing Corporation.
Bohnet, Iris. 2018. *WORK DESIGN: Kodo Keizai-gaku de Gender Gakusa o Kokufuku suru* [What works: Gender equality by design] 2016, trans. Chiaki Ikemura. NTT Publishing Co., Ltd.
Bourdieu, Pierre. 1991. *Kozo to Jissen: Bourdieu Jishin niyoru Bourdieu* [Choses Dites] 1987, trans. Harumi Ishizaki. Fujiwara-Shoten.
Fisman, Raymond, and Edward Miguel. 2014. *Warui Yatsuhodo Goriteki: Fuhai, Kenryoku, Hinkon no Keizai-gaku* [Economic gangsters: Corruption, violence, and the poverty of nations] 2008, trans. Tetsuro Mizoguchi and Katsuyoshi Tamura. NTT Publishing Co., Ltd.
Gneezy, Uri., and John List. 2014. *Sono Mondai Keizai-gaku de Kaiketsu Dekimasu* [The why axis: Hidden motives and the undiscovered economics of everyday life] 2013, trans. Mamoru Mochizuki. Toyo Keizai Inc.
Greif, Avner. 2009. *Hikaku Rekishi Seido Bunseki* [Institutions and the path to the modern economy: Lessons from medieval trade: Political economy of institutions and decisions], trans. Michihiro Kandori and Tetsuji Okazaki. NTT Publishing Co., Ltd.
Heckman, James. 2015. *Yoji Kyoiku no Keizai-gaku* [Giving kids a fair chance: A strategy that works] 2013, trans. Hideko Furukusa. Toyo Keizai Inc.
Keynes, John Maynard. (1959). *Jinbutsu Hyoden* [Essays in biography] 1951, trans. Hisao Kumagai and Tadao Ono. Iwanami Shoten, Publishers.
Leeson, Peter. 2011. *Kaizoku no Keizai-gaku: Miezaru Hook no Himitsu* [The invisible hook: The hidden economics of pirates] 2009, trans. Hiroo Yamagata. NTT Publishing Co., Ltd.
Levitt, Steven D., and Stephen J. Dubner. 2006. *Yabai Keizai-gaku: Warugaki Kyoju ga Yo no Ura o Tanken suru* [Freakonomics: A rogue economist explores the hidden side of everything] 2005, trans. Mamoru Mochizuki. Toyo Keizai Inc.
Nisbett, Richard E., and Dov Cohen. 2009. *Meiyo to Boryoku: America Nambu no Bunka to Shinri* [Culture of honor: The psychology of violence in the South] 1996, trans. Keiko Ishii and Masaki Yuki. Kitaooji Shobo Publishing.
Piketty, Thomas. 2014. *21-seiki no Shihon-shugi* [Le Capital au XXIe siècle] 2013, trans. Hiroo Yamagata, Sakura Morioka, and Masafumi Morimoto. Misuzu Shobo.
Powell, Benjamin. (2016). *Imin No Keizai-gaku* [The economics of immigration] 2015, trans. Shiro Yabushita. Toyo Keizai Inc.
Saint-Exupery, Antoine de. 2006. *Hoshi no Ouji sama* [Le Petit Prince] 1943. Translated by Mariko Kono. Shinchosha.
van den Boom, Maike. 2016. *Sekai Kofuku Ranking Joi 13 ka koku o Tabishite Wakatta koto* [Wo geht's denn hier zum Glück?: Meine Reise durch die 13 glücklichsten Ländern der Welt und was wir von ihnen lernen können] 2015, trans. Tsukasa Azegami. Shueisya Inc.
Vance, James David. 2017. *Hillbilly Elegy: America no Han-ei kara torinoko-sareta Hakujin-tachi* [Hillbilly elegy: A memoir of a family and culture in crisis] 2016, trans. Mitsuhiro Sekine and Aya Yamada. Kobunsha Co., Ltd.

Literature in English

Abramitzky, R., L. Einav, and O. Rigbi. 2010. Is Hanukkah responsive to Christmas? *Economic Journal* 120: 612–630.
Akerlof, G.A., and R.E. Kranton. 2000. Economics and identity. *Quarterly Journal of Economics* 115: 715–753.
Algan, Y., and P. Cahuc. 2010. Inherited trust and growth. *American Economic Review* 100 (5): 2060–2092.
Algan, Y., P. Cahuc, and A. Shleifer. 2013. Teaching practices and social capital. *American Economic Journal: Applied Economics* 5 (3): 189–210.
Andreoni, J. 1989. Giving with impure altruism: Application to charity and Ricardian equivalence. *Journal of Political Economics* 97 (6): 1447–1458.
Andreoni, J. 1990. Impure altruism and donations to public goods: A theory of warm-glow giving. *Economic Journal* 100 (401): 464–477.
Becker, G.S., and K.M. Murphy. 1988. A theory of rational addiction. *Journal of Political Economy* 96 (4): 675–700.
Benedict, Ruth. 1946. *The Chrysanthemum and the sword*. Patterns of Japanese culture. Albatross Publishers, Tokyo.
Bateson, M., D. Nettle, and G. Roberts. 2012. Cycle thieves, we are watching you: Impact of a simple signage intervention against bicycle. *Plos ONE* 7 (12).
Booth, A., and E. Yamamura. 2018. Performance in mixed-sex and single-sex tournaments: What we can learn from speedboat races in Japan. *Review of Economics & Statistics* 100 (4): 581–593.
Borowiecki, Karol J. 2017. How are you, my dearest Mozart? Well-being and creativity of three famous composers based on their letters. *Review of Economics and Statistics* 99 (4): 591–605.
Borrell-Porta, M., J. Costa-Font, and J. Philipp. 2019. The 'mighty girl' effect; does parenting daughters alter attitudes towards gender norm? *Oxford Economic Papers* 71 (1): 25–46.
Byun, S. K., and J. M. Oh. 2018. Local corporate social responsibility, media coverage, and shareholder value. *Journal of Banking & Finance* 87 (C), 68–86.
Cronqvist, H., and F. Yu. 2017. Shaped by their daughters: Executives, female socialization, and corporate social responsibility. *Journal of Financial Economics* 126 (3): 543–562.
Fernandez, R., A. Fogli, and C. Olivetti. 2004. Mothers and sons: Preference formation and female labor force dynamics. *Quarterly Journal of Economics* 119, 1249–1299
Granovetter, M. 1973. The strength of weak ties. *American Journal of Sociology* 78 (6): 1360–1380.
Giuliano, P., and A. Spilimbergo. 2014. Growing up in a recession. *Review of Economic Studies* 81 (2): 787–817.
Ito, T., K. Kubota, and Ohtake, F. 2021. The hidden curriculum and social preferences. Forthcoming in *Japanese Economic Review*.
Kawaguchi, D., and J. Miyazaki. 2009. Working mothers and sons' preferences regarding female labor supply: Direct evidence from stated preferences. *Journal of Population Economics* 22 (1): 115–130.
Luttmer, E. 2005. Neighbors as negatives: Relative earnings and well-being. *Quarterly Journal of Economics* 120: 963–1002.
Maystre, N., J. Olivier, M. Thoenig, and T. Verdier. 2014. Product-based cultural changes: Is the village global? *Journal of International Economics* 92: 212–230.
Munshi, K. 2003. Networks in the modern economy: Mexican migrants in the U. S. labor market. *Quarterly Journal of Economics* 118 (2), 549–599.
Oswald, A.J., and N. Powdthavee. 2010. Daughters and left-wing voting. *Review of Economics and Statistics* 92: 213–227.
Piketty, T. 1995. Social mobility and redistributive politics. *Quarterly Journal of Economics* 110 (3): 551–584.
Washington, E. 2008. Female socialization: How daughters affect their legislator fathers' voting on women's issues. *American Economic Review* 98: 311–332.

Yamamura, E. 2008. Socio-economic effects on increased cinema attendance: The case of Japan. *Journal of Socio-Economics* 37 (6): 2546–2555.

Yamamura, E. 2009a. Dynamics of social trust and human capital in the learning process: The case of the Japan garment cluster in the period 1968–2005. *Journal of Economic Behavior and Organization* 72 (1), 377–389.

Yamamura, E. 2009b. Rethinking rational addictive behavior and demand for cinema: A study using Japanese panel data. *Applied Economics Letters* 16 (7), 693–697.

Yamamura, E. 2010. How do female spouses' political interests affect male spouses' views about a women's issue? *Atlantic Economic Journal* 38 (3): 359–370.

Yamamura, E. 2011a. Game information, local heroes, and their effect on attendance: The case of the Japanese baseball league. *Journal of Sports Economics* 12: 20–35.

Yamamura, E. 2011b. The role of social trust in reducing long-term truancy and forming human capital in Japan. *Economics of Education Review* 30 (2): 380–389.

Yamamura, E. 2011c. The effects of the social norm on cigarette consumption: Evidence from Japan using panel data. *Japan & World Economy* 23 (1): 6–12.

Yamamura, E. 2012a. Social capital, household income, and preferences for income redistribution. *European Journal of Political Economy* 28 (4), 498–511.

Yamamura, E. 2012b. The effect of social trust on achievement test performance of students in Japan. *Applied Economics Letters* 19 (7), 645–648.

Yamamura, E. 2012c. Effect of Linguistic Heterogeneity on Technology Transfer: An Economic Study of FIFA Football Rankings. *Atlantic Economic Journal* 40 (1), 85–99.

Yamamura, E. 2012d. Charitable giving under inequality aversion and social capital. *Economics Bulletin* 32 (4), 3140–3147.

Yamamura, E. 2014. The effect of young children on their parents' anime viewing habits: Evidence from Japanese micro data. *Journal of Cultural Economics* 38 (4): 331–449.

Yamamura, E. 2015. Wage disparity and team performance in the process of industry development. *Journal of Sports Economics* 16 (2): 214–223.

Yamamura, E. 2017. Identity, nostalgia and happiness among migrants: The case of the Kōshien High School Baseball Tournament in Japan. *Pacific Economic Review* 22 (5): 792–813.

Yamamura, E. 2019. Gender wage gap and its effect on test scores of immigrant students. *Journal of Economic Studies* 46 (4): 872–887.

Yamamura, E., and Y. Mano. 2012. An investigation into the positive effect of an educated wife on her husband's earnings. *International Advances in Economic Research* 18 (4): 409–416.

Yamamura, E., and I. Shin. 2016. Effect of consuming imported cultural goods on trading partners' tolerance toward immigrants: The case of Japanese anime in Korea. *Review of World Economics* 152 (4): 681–703.

Yamamura, E., and Y. Tsutsui. 2017a. Comparing the role of height between men and women in the marriage market. *Economics and Human Biology* 26: 42–50.

Yamamura, E., and Y. Tsutsui. 2017b. Gap of height and education within couple and its effect on conflict and evaluation about partners: Psychological cost of division of labor within household. Discussion Papers in Economics and Business 17–35, Osaka School of International Public Policy (OSIPP).

Yamamura, E., and Y. Tsutsui. 2019a. Trade policy preference, childhood sporting experience, and informal school curriculum: an examination of views of the TPP from the viewpoint of behavioral economics. *Review of International Economics* 27(1), 61–90.

Yamamura, E., and Tsutsui, Y. 2019b. Effects of pregnancy and birth on smoking and drinking behaviours: A comparative study between men and women. *Japanese Economic Review* 70 (2), 210–234.

Yamamura, E., and Y. Tsutsui. 2021. Spousal gaps in age and identity, and their impact on the allocation of housework. *Empirical Economics* 60 (2): 1059–1083.

Yamamura, E., Y. Tsutsui, & S. Managi. 2019. Male pupils taught by female homeroom teachers show higher preference for Corporate Social Responsibility in adulthood. *Journal of Japanese and International Economies* 54 (C).

Yamamura, E., Y. Tsutsui, and O. Ohtake. 2021. Altruistic and selfish motivations of charitable giving: Case of the hometown tax donation system in Japan. Forthcoming in *Japanese Economic Review*.

Zak, P. 2012. *The moral molecule. How trust works*. New York: Penguin Group.

GPSR Compliance

The European Union's (EU) General Product Safety Regulation (GPSR) is a set of rules that requires consumer products to be safe and our obligations to ensure this.

If you have any concerns about our products, you can contact us on

ProductSafety@springernature.com

In case Publisher is established outside the EU, the EU authorized representative is:

Springer Nature Customer Service Center GmbH
Europaplatz 3
69115 Heidelberg, Germany